Samuel Colcord Bartlett

Sources of History in the Pentateuch

Six Lectures Delivered in the Theological Seminary

Samuel Colcord Bartlett

Sources of History in the Pentateuch
Six Lectures Delivered in the Theological Seminary

ISBN/EAN: 9783337172695

Printed in Europe, USA, Canada, Australia, Japan

Cover: Foto ©Lupo / pixelio.de

More available books at **www.hansebooks.com**

SOURCES OF HISTORY

IN THE

PENTATEUCH

SIX LECTURES DELIVERED IN PRINCETON THEO-
LOGICAL SEMINARY, ON THE STONE
FOUNDATION, MARCH, 1882

BY

SAMUEL C. BARTLETT, D.D., LL.D.
President of Dartmouth College

NEW YORK
ANSON D. F. RANDOLPH & COMPANY
900 BROADWAY, COR. 20th STREET

Copyright, 1883,
BY ANSON D. F. RANDOLPH & COMPANY

ST. JOHNLAND
STEREOTYPE FOUNDRY,
SUFFOLK CO., N. Y.

PRINTED BY
EDWARD O. JENKINS,
20 NORTH WILLIAM ST., N. Y.

CONTENTS.

LECTURE FIRST.
THE EARLIEST COSMOGONY 1

LECTURE SECOND.
EARLY MAN 36

LECTURE THIRD.
THE EARLY ARTS 76

LECTURE FOURTH.
THE EARLY CONSANGUINITIES 116

LECTURE FIFTH.
THE EARLY MOVEMENTS OF THE NATIONS . . 148

LECTURE SIXTH.
THE EARLY DOCUMENTS 180

APPENDIX.
EXTRACT FROM STRACK ON THE PENTATEUCH . 217

SOURCES OF HISTORY IN THE PENTATEUCH.

LECTURE FIRST.

THE EARLIEST COSMOGONY.

The five books of Moses, like the Revelation of which they form the grand propylæum, have in our day been chiefly put upon the defensive. As many a writer, indebted to the Christian system for his ethics, has received the gift and disparaged the source, so have a large class of investigators gained invaluable and indispensable aid from the Pentateuch, and then endeavored to use its own frank utterances to invalidate its authority. And so the portico has been viewed rather as a beleagured fortress.

I propose in this brief course of lectures to abandon the negative position and set forth in the direct and affirmative aspect the claims of the Pentateuch as a book of origins, containing the sources of all our earliest consecutive knowledge, and alone solving those great questions concerning the human race which must be asked and which lie otherwise unanswered. While an unparalleled assiduity and variety of research are enlarging the boundaries of our knowledge of the past, and a marvellous ingenuity is unlocking the historic secrets which seemed to have perished with their original possessors, it remains none the less true that these results are fragmentary and often incoherent, till they are laid beside the one central and continuous story. This is the substantive account, they are the adjuncts. For unexplored centuries down to the time of him who is called the Father of History, the Pentateuch walks alone but with unfaltering step over the pathway of the past. And it is beginning to appear more and more clearly, as I shall attempt incidentally to show, that our function is not to defend it, much less to apologize for it, but to unfold, explain and follow its guidance, properly understood, in the well-grounded assurance that it will give more light than it receives from these modern researches, that they are to be brought thither in good degree to be tested, and that they must be laid beside it in order to give them any complete coherence and valid significance. And in a great measure their use is to serve as furnishing the illustrative facts, whereby its brief statements and often obscure hints shall be clearly understood. In discussing this subject it is inevitable to begin with the familiar if not hackneyed theme of THE EARLIEST COSMOGONY. The discussion is by no means superfluous. For perhaps no theme has suffered more in the handling, whether from friendly or hostile pens. Largely, if not chiefly, from misapprehension of the aim and method.

All fair criticism of any composition must proceed from a recognition not only of its nature, as poetry, philosophy, narrative and the like, but, if it be history, of the class for whom it is written, the end in view, and therefore the method adopted. To deal fairly with the Creation-narrative such consideration is absolutely indispensable. I address myself therefore first to these questions. What then is the nature of the composition?

Now, then, it is idle to designate this simple record as anything else than a narrative. To call it a parable as some have done, or a psalm of Creation with others, is doing violence to the most obvious facts. There are psalms of Creation, pre-eminently the one hundred and fourth psalm, which, as Von Humboldt[1] has well said, represents "the image of the Cosmos," sketching with a few bold touches the whole universe, the heavens and the earth. That is manifestly poetry. But if any records in the Old Testament read like plain veritable history, the first chapter of Genesis surely is one of them. Nothing could be more sober, simple, matter-of-fact.

But for whom was it written? For no one class, but for all classes, ages, races, conditions,—for mankind. This fact carries consequences.

With what aim was it written? Clearly, not for its own separate value, but as a needful brief introduction to the revelation of God for man's redemption,—a preliminary explanation. Again, not chiefly for his intellectual education, but for his moral enlightenment and religious impression; not for completeness of science, but for the uses of duty and piety. This too carries consequences.

These and other considerations fix our attention on the *method* of the narrative—a matter of vital importance for its right interpretation. A failure to recognize distinctly the writer's method is wholly to lose the clue to any right apprehension or even fair treatment of the record.

[1] Humboldt's "Cosmos," ii. pp. 58-9 (Am. Trans.)

(1.) The first fact of method that we are bound to consider, is its singular, I might well say, its amazing brevity. The narrative is here foreshortened to an unparalleled degree. Some thirty short verses are made to contain the whole formation of this universe, from its inception to its completion. Now casting aside all the wilder claims sometimes made for hundreds and thousands of millions of years[2] since life began, and taking the more moderate estimate of Sir William Thomson, some years ago, of from seventy to one hundred millions of years,[3] or the later and much more moderate estimate of Tait[4] which gives from ten to fifteen millions as the past limit of the present order of things—the time since the globe became fitted for the existence of life—or the later estimate of Professor C. A. Young[5] which assigns eighteen millions

[2] Thus Haeckel: "The organic history of the earth must not be calculated by thousands of years, but by palæontological or geological periods, *each of which* comprises many thousands of years and perhaps even millions or *milliards of thousands* of years." "It is most advisable from a philosophical point of view to conceive this period of creation to be as long as possible" ("History of Creation," ii. p. 337).

[3] Geike in his "Geology" (London, 1882, p. 55,) still favors "not much less than a hundred million years."

[4] "Recent Advances of Physical Science," p. 167.

[5] "The Sun," p. 277.

of years as the longest limit of the past duration of the solar system, we should have on the highest estimate, an average of from three to five millions of years, and on the lowest estimate, of half a million of years, to a verse. What an unexampled compression! Suppose a writer were required distinctly and vividly to set forth the history of the world for six thousand years, or of Europe for nineteen hundred, or of America for two hundred and fifty, in the compass of thirty sentences, what would be the result? I can think of nothing whereby to illustrate the process so effectually as an attempt to draw a map of North America in the space of a square inch. Consider how details must disappear; rivers, mountains and lakes of great magnitude are wholly lost; the manifold indentations of the coast give way to straight or slightly bent lines; and a few brief strokes of the pencil take the place of an indefinite amount and variety of configurations. It is but an outline sketch,—correct but necessarily incomplete. Now in like manner the exceeding brevity of this narrative necessitates (*a*) the omission and disregard of details. It is and can be but a graphic outline sketch, drawn with bold characterizing strokes, overlooking all minor particulars, even all modifying qualifications and minute exceptions. This fact at once obviates the necessity and propriety of dealing with and looking for any but the great characterizing features. If, for example, some lower (marsupial)[6] form of mammal life anticipated the great outburst of mammals upon the earth we can no more expect that the narrative should specify it than that our square-inch map should recognize Currituck Inlet or Cape Ann. The only expansion it admits is the rhetorical fulness of expression which shall make clear, impressive and vivid its sweeping outline statements.

This brevity carries another feature, viz., (*b*) a continuous forward movement and final dismissal of facts once narrated in their order. This is a feature of the narrative most important to be recognized. It passes steadily on from stage to stage, with the successive steps, or rather germs of progress. It marks the *initiation* of one stage of the creation, then proceeds to another, but never afterwards resumes its account of the former though it may have been a long-continued process, not intermitted even when another supervenes. The narrative describes each new movement in succession, and then dismisses it finally.

[6] *e. g.*, The Microlestes and Dromatherium, marsupials and therefore semiviviparous, in the Trias.

And from this fact follows another noticeable and important feature of the narrative, viz., (*c*) that the announcement and dismissal of a given set of phenomena,—any distinct branch of the creative work,—seeing that it is not to be resumed and further narrated in the sequel, is summed up and described *as a whole*, in its completeness. It is the briefest possible method of dispatching the subject. This fact meets us unmistakably in regard to the formation of the continents and the vegetable system, in regard to the introduction of all the various forms of life, and even, as we have reason to believe, in reference to the functions of the heavenly bodies,—each of which processes was the work of long ages.

This singular condensation, with its three subordinate points, of grand characterization with omission of details, steady forward movement without recapitulation, and the summing up and dismissal of each branch of the process, announced in its totality and completeness, removes nearly all the real and serious difficulties of the narration. Other less serious, though more obvious occasions of questioning are met by considering,

(2.) Another governing quality of method, viz., its design to be intelligible to the human race. This purpose carries by necessity certain qualities which require only to be mentioned, to be recognized: (*a*) the narrative is, as a description, thoroughly popular and not in the slightest degree scientific. It sets forth obvious and recognizable results, and makes no attempt at a scientific account of the processes. A statement of the scientific aspects of the case, had it been revealed to the narrator, would have found, for more than three thousand years, not only no person capable of comprehending, but none capable of receiving it. Such a narrative would have been, down to the present century, a hopeless stumbling-block at the threshold of the sacred word. But the sacred history avoids everything that is scientific, and is, as was indispensable, completely popular in its method. And one very noticeable aspect of the narrative viewed in this light is that, instead of fixing the attention upon the *process*, it describes quite commonly by the *result*,—that result being often simple enough of recognition as a mere outward *sign*, but marking changes the most immense and stupendous,—such changes as must have preceded the appearance of a visible welkin, or the disclosure of sun, moon and stars. (*b*) Another kindred feature is the necessary absence of everything like a technical term. The Hebrew language, in-

deed, offered no such mechanism of speech.
If the case had been otherwise, it would have
been wholly alien from the writer's aim and
method. The narrative throughout is clothed
with all the drapery and attractiveness of the
language and scenery of human life and action. We have no universe, το πᾶν or τα
πάντα, but "the heavens and the earth"; no
mammals, but "cattle and creeping thing and
beast of the earth"; no atmosphere (as Gaussen[7]
would find in the "firmament"), but simply
"heaven," or the visible sky; no chaos, but
"emptiness and desolation" (Hebrew); no
cosmic gas, nor chemical elements uncon-
densed and uncombined, but "the deep"; no
molecular action, but the "brooding" of God's
spirit. When the grains and the fruit-trees
are described as bearing "after their kind"
it is therefore simply characterizing by the
most obvious marks, and no assertion, as some
unwisely claim, of any recondite doctrine of
immutability of species. Nor can we fairly
find, even with the eminent Benjamin Pierce,
the "light" put as a representative of "the
forces of Nature"—a scientific conception. It
stands simply for itself,—light. God himself,
instead of putting forth volitions, "says," as
though audibly speaking, "let there be light";

[7] Gaussen, "The World's Birth Day," pp. 93 seq.

he gives names to the objects; he communes with himself; he contemplates the results with satisfaction, pronouncing them "good," "very good." It is all part of the graphic, untechnical, human method, which should meet the apprehension and arrest the attention of any and every member of the human race. And it is strictly in keeping with this same method, that the several stages of the creative process are represented under the vivid aspect of so many successive day's works of the Creator, —which, as Bunsen suggests,[8] is the simplest mode of viewing the whole matter. And thus instead of geological epoch or era, for which the Hebrew language offered no phraseology and the human mind for many thousand years no receptivity, we have God's "day," the vast extent of which the researches of future ages alone should unfold. But of this more in the sequel. (c). Another obvious as well as needful aspect of this method, is that it is purely a *phenomenal* description. All is represented as it appeared, or would have appeared, to the eye of the beholder. And this fact has even suggested to Godet, Kurtz, Miller and others, the idea of an original revelation in vision, by a series of what might be called dioramic representations passing before the

[8] "Bibelwerk," Gen. i. 5.

mental eye, opened and closed by its succession of darkness and light. Such a supposition, though not an impossible one, and though in some respects facilitating the explanation, is by no means necessary. It is enough to recognize the unmistakable fact that the description is phenomenal—not necessarily visional, but chiefly visual or optical. This feature appears beyond question in the case of the heavenly bodies, described not as they are, the sun a luminary, the moon a reflecting satellite, but as they appear in the heavens, the one to rule the day, the other the night. This indeed may be emphasized as a test case in regard to the character of the whole narrative. But the same characteristic appears more or less clearly in all the other parts of the history—the visible heaven dividing waters from waters, the obvious distinctions of the forms of vegetation, the "stretched out" creatures, the winged creatures flying "*on the face*" (Hebrew) of the expanse of heaven, and "everything that *creepeth* upon the earth,"—for so they look upon the great globe—all of it phenomenal and even pictorial.

All these qualities of method grow so naturally out of the aim of the narrator, and lie so manifestly on the face of the narrative, that when once clearly stated, they cannot fail to be recognized as alike true and important. But the actual non-recognition of them has been the constant stumbling-block. No intelligent apprehension and no fair and candid treatment of the narrative can overlook their bearing. We might as well ignore the dramatic character of Job or the figurative phraseology of the Biblical poetry. This is narrative, history,—but narrative written in a thoroughly popular style and method, in order to reach all men. I lay all emphasis on these several principles, because in them lies the clue to the whole narrative; and its proper interpretation comes from their application.

Applying now these true and simple principles to the narrative, how readily we bring out in this record, made in the comparative infancy of the world, the sharp bold outline sketch, of which the world in its supposed maturity has only within a century been able to supply the multitudinous and often confused details, and by laying them beside that original sketch, so clear that all the world has understood it in every essential feature, find that there lay the true germ and outline of the whole. The chief liability to inadequate conception was on the one point of the lapse of time,—a point on which all conception is inadequate, and on which it would have been not only needless, but worse than useless, to attempt conveying an approximate impression in advance of the slow gropings and discoveries of investigation. Yet even here the account is not destitute of clear hints by which bright minds like Augustine's long ago profited, to see that the "day" of God's working was of unknown duration, and might be to man's day somewhat in the ratio of God to man.[9]

Shall I now rapidly unfold this sketch of creation in the double light of its own obvious plan of description, and the latest results of investigation.

"The beginning" was evidently prior to all existences in this universe of ours, except that of God the Creator. The "heavens and the earth" are clearly the visible universe. "Creation" in the first verse cannot well be understood of anything short of absolute origination, not alone or chiefly (1) because the

---

[9] Says Augustine: "What kind of days they are is either very difficult or quite impossible for us to think, much more to express. For we see that the days we know have their evening only by the setting of the sun, and their morning by its rising. But the first three were spent without the sun, which is related to have been made on the fourth" ("*Civitate Dei,*" xi. 6, 7).

Hebrew בָּרָא is the proper word to express such a thought, even more specific than the English "create," being used forty-eight times in the Kal conjugation and always having God for its subject, never accompanied with an accusative of material, and being employed to describe the Divine production, in the kingdom of nature or of grace, of what had no existence before, nor even alone (2) because such is apparently the exposition given in Heb. xi. 3; but necessarily (3) by the exigencies of the narrative—inasmuch as every plastic process is subsequently described, and so exhaustively as to leave nothing for the "creation" except origination of the material. If it be said that the absolute origination of matter passes all comprehension and conception, we reply, of course, so do all things ultimate; and it is, so to speak, less incomprehensible that an almighty power could originate it, than that an inert material could have been self-existent, self-originated, or eternal.

It is important to observe that the second verse cuts clear of the universe at large, or even of the solar system, and confines itself to "the earth." This fact would seem to preclude the view advanced by so high scientific authorities as Guyot and Dana, that in a subsequent verse the dividing of the waters from the waters was the separation of the earth from the nebula of which it was a part, and forces us to a simpler and narrower explanation. "The earth"—to which our attention is now confined—was after its creation "without form and void," literally "wasteness and emptiness," in other words a chaotic mass, described by two archaic Hebrew words, תֹּהוּ וָבֹהוּ, and in the next breath designated as "the deep"; perhaps because no other than this last term could so vividly describe the vast, confused, unstable and, it may be, heaving and roaring mass of material in its earlier stages, as the vast ocean abyss. For "the spirit of God" at length "moved" or rather *brooded* upon it, began a steady and long continued agency,—there being no necessity of limiting this process to the initial stage, inasmuch as the word "brood" hints otherwise. And in this "brooding," the chaos deep is now described as "the waters," a phrase which both retains the figure of the ocean and may suggest the mobile, not to say fluid, condition of the material, which scientists affirm to have been once gaseous or nebulous. There was a stage when all was darkness; then came the creation of light, "offspring of heaven first born." Nothing would help us to explain the whole transaction recorded in a single verse

(3rd) so well as the acceptance not alone of the nebular theory—though not cleared of all objections, *e. g.*, the lack of certain elements in the sun which are prominent in the earth, —but even of the plausible speculations of Lockyer, viz., that "the chemical elements themselves are one kind of matter under differently aggregated forms, at first diffused through the universe; that atom coalesced with atom, singly or in groups, and that the most primitive of our elements, such as hydrogen, were formed. Further and further aggregations took place, the equally diffused matter became more and more condensed, in certain parts forming distinct nebulæ, which went on shrinking more and more, and increasing in density as they diminished in size, until, to take a single instance, the matter which uniformly filled a space much greater than the entire solar system, became condensed into the bodies of the sun and planets, leaving between them only that thin impalpable substance to which we give the name of ether. The shock of the atoms as they struck against each other, not only gave them a motion of revolution, but raised them to a temperature of which we have scarcely any conception, and which rendered the existence not only of compounds, but of many of the actual metals themselves, impossible."[10] This would help us, if we might accept it, though it is not indispensable.

Fixing now the attention on the supposed stage of the process when the great chemical combination and condensation began in good earnest, accompanied by an intense and inconceivable heat—when the material of our earth suddenly shrank from what Dawson suggests[11] as two thousand times its present diameter towards some approximation to its present dimensions—and you have now that intense molecular activity which, as Professor Dana remarks, "would show itself instantly by a manifestation of light," and "a flash of light through the universe would be the first announcement of the work begun."

But observe that the statement, "there was light," gives a fact that is not so much significant for itself as in its being the sign, the remarkable sign, of the most enormous changes not otherwise set forth. This, it will be observed again, is characteristic of the whole narrative. The existence of light before the manifestation of the sun, and independent of it, was the stumbling-block of Voltaire a cen-

---

[10] Brunton's "Science and the Bible," p. 340–1.
[11] "Story of the Earth and Man," p. 9.

tury since, and of an English churchman [12] but twenty years ago, but offers no difficulty to a well taught school-boy. This sudden breaking in of light upon the scene of long preceding darkness, like an evening followed by a morning, falls in with, perhaps gives rise to, the imagery of a divine day's work, thenceforward maintained through the narrative,—although afterwards the terms morning and evening are perhaps generalized to denote the beginning and ending of a formative period, or (Lange) "the interval of a creative day." That this word "day" does not signify a solar day we are warned by the fact stated in the narrative, that the solar day was not yet provided for, a fact which long ago intimated to such minds as Augustine's and Bede's [13] that a solar day was not intended. When the narrative ascribes the formation of the oceans and continents to a part of one day, it therein describes a fact which by the laws of hydrostatics could not completely take place in any

[12] C. A. Goodwin, Oxford, "Essays and Reviews," p. 246.
[13] Says Bede (Comment. in Pentateuchum, Vol. ii. p. 194, Migne), "'Unus dies.' Fortassis hic diei nomen totius temporis nomen est, et omnia volumina sæculorum hoc vocabulo includit." In his Hexaemeron (i. D.) he speaks however as though the day were of twenty-four hours accomplished by the going and coming of the light, as now of the sun.

part of a solar day. When it employs this word "day" with four, if not five different applications, in this one narrative (vs. 5, 14, ii. 4), it thereby warns against the possibility of confining it to this one narrow meaning.[14] When it mentions God's "day" of rest from creating, it mentions a day which has continued now for many thousand years, and constrains us by the rules of consistency to recognize also his creative days as protracted periods. The Biblical idiom and the popular speech of man alike justify an indefinite extension of the terms,[15] such as the discoveries of science compel. If it be said that the closing consecration of the seventh day proves that we are dealing only with a solar day, we answer, the consecration of our seventh day does not necessarily identify the actual length of God's and man's day of rest, but only the ratio in the two cases; as God's resting day to his working days, so is man's resting day to his working days, the seventh to each of the six. The whole series of events was on a

[14] In verse fifth it designates the total succession of light and darkness when there was no sun, and also the light portion of that period; in verse fourteenth, the solar day, and also the light portion of that day; in ch. ii. 4, apparently, the whole time of the creation.

[15] Day of salvation, visitation, prosperity, adversity; his day, my day, etc.

colossal scale to which all terms of actual measurement are alike inadequate. And in treating this topic I prefer saying that *the whole process* is represented under *the figure* of a series of day's works, rather than to insist solely on a flexible use of the word "day"—though the latter is a tenable position.[16]

It may be added that the whole aim and instruction of the narrative were subserved just as well by leaving for the future unfoldings of exploration, the incomprehensible, and, till recently, incredible length of these periods of creation. The attempted disclosure would even have marred the influence and the usefulness of the narrative.

We can proceed more rapidly. The second day is marked by the "firmament"—the expanse—explained in the record as being called heaven. The visible sky, the blue welkin, is here designated,—not (with Gaussen) the atmosphere,—which would be too scientific. And the waters below are the ocean, now at length able

---

[16] Thus, though the case is not fully parallel, I would say that the parable of the unjust judge sets forth God's accessibleness to importunate prayer; but here, plainly, we cannot properly say that God is represented as an unjust judge.

On the ratio of God's days and man's, see Reusch, "Bibel und Natur," p. 128. Bonn, 1876.

to lie on the cooler crust of the earth, while the waters above, the clouds, are seen floating, separated by the visible expanse. For the רָקִיעַ is not the *firmamentum* of the Vulgate (something hammered *solid*,) but something hammered out *thin*, spread out, an expanse. But observe that this visible sky, with the waters lying beneath and floating aloft, is, like the "light" of the previous day, but the recognizable and obvious *sign* of untold, enormous changes which have meanwhile gone forward. There has been an amazing condensation and combination of elements, inconceivable heat and incandescence of a gaseous and molten mass, a long cooling off[17] till at length the surface is lower than the temperature 212 degrees, and the disengagement of a surrounding atmosphere, widely different from that of to-day, yet such that while a universal ocean swathes the earth (as science also affirms), dense vapors are borne aloft. All this vast history, as we now know, is indicated, or covered up by the simple mention of this visible sign, a sky with waters above and below it; just as we answer the question, how cold is

---

[17] Dana mentions that Helmholtz demands three hundred and fifty millions of years for the cooling from 2000 degrees to 200 degrees Fahrenheit. "Geology," p. 147. The statement is given as a curiosity. "The estimate of another author," says Dana "is four times this."

the day, by giving the visible sign,—the mercury stands at —20 degrees. Such is the method.

The next stage of progress, the third day, is indicated by two grand strokes of the pencil or pen. First the formation of the continents, accompanied by the withdrawal of the ocean to its bed; a process now well known to have preceded all further development. The cooling earth wrinkled its huge folds and reared the oldest mountain chains. Here observe the method. This new order of things —the change—is stated once for all, and, with this brief announcement, dismissed; although the process continued through succeeding ages usually reckoned as millions of years. The first continents were, comparatively speaking, meagre strips of land. In North America the chief original nucleus, the oldest known rocks, ("not the absolute oldest," Le Conte) lay in the British Provinces, with the outlying Adirondacks, part of the Appalachian line, islands in New England, patches in Nova Scotia and New Brunswick, a Pacific coast range in Mexico, and various detached areas in the Mississippi basin west, as the Black Hills of Dakota. The European Continent was chiefly an archipelago as late as the Devonian era (Dana). But since their first emergence the continents have been enlarging and the mountains rising—the Rocky mountains not less than eleven thousand feet in the Tertiary age; and the period of comparative rest seems not to have been reached till since the great glacial epoch. But the narrative has done with it in the first and final announcement.[18]

The other event of this third day was the introduction of vegetable life. The fragile nature of plants, and especially of the earliest, taken in connection with the vast vicissitudes since those remotest eras, is a good reason why they are not found in proper form so far back as the narrative requires. But the scientific probability, if not certainty, of their existence antecedent, as a whole, to that of animal life, appears from the facts (1) that "a

---

[18] Thus, Le Conte affirms that the end of the Cretaceous was "pre-eminently a time of continent-making," there occurring at that time "a bodily upheaval of the whole western half of the [American] continent, by which the great interior sea which previously divided America into two continents was abolished, and the continent became one." So also "the end of the Jurassic had been pre-eminently a time of mountain-making" ("Geology," p. 475). Dana carries out this last point in detail ("Geol." p. 754) by estimating (on the basis of forty-eight millions of years from the beginning of the Silurian period to the present) that the interval from the beginning of the Primordial "to the uplifts and metamorphism of the Green mountains was 20,000,000 years and to the completion of the Alleghanies 36,000,000."

temperature admitting of the existence of vegetation would have been reached, in the process of refrigeration, before that of animal life:" (2) that animals require plants for food, finding no nutriment in inorganic matter; (3) and still more positively from the immense amount of graphite with its carbon and of iron ore far down in the Laurentian rocks, (and in Europe anthracite,) implying former vegetable life.[19] So say the geologists. As the earliest vegetables appear to have been sea-weeds, their relics could not be expected in any more defined condition.

Here we meet one of the few, at first sight, *serious* difficulties. The writer describes the whole vegetable world, including "the herb yielding seed and the fruit tree yielding fruit." But we find by exploration that these belong mostly to a very late period of the geological history, some of them not long antedating the human race. How is this? The answer is very simple. Just as in the case of the continents, and later in regard to the forms of animal life, the writer despatches the whole

[19] Dana, "Geology,' p. 157. Le Conte, "Geology," p. 274. Geike, "Geology," p. 639. Geike says, "Dr. Sterry Hunt has called attention to these [iron] ores as proving the precipitation of iron by decomposing vegetation on a more gigantic scale than at any subsequent geological epoch."

subject with one stroke. Since he will not recur to the fact, he describes in its completeness that of which he now narrates the inception, and so dismisses it finally. This is his method.

But for a long time after the simpler forms of vegetation were possible, the geologist has shown us that the atmosphere and the earth's surface were in a very different condition from their present state, and wholly unfitted for the present forms of animal life. Not only must the higher temperature have filled the air constantly with a vast amount of watery vapor, wrapping it (to use the figure of Le Conte,) as in a double blanket, and making of it a great conservatory or forcing hothouse, but it was loaded with all the carbon that is now embedded in the coal formation and the marble and limestone rocks, the chlorine and sulphurous acids of the various chlorides and sulphurets and sulphurs of the earth's surface—"an atmosphere," says Sterry Hunt "charged with acid gasses, and of immense density."[20]

The fourth day's work is characterized by the eventful fact that at length the light of the heavenly bodies found its way through and shone upon the earth. This again is but

[20] Lecture before the Royal Institution of London, 1867

the striking *sign* of vast intervening but undescribed changes, that had taken place on the earth's surface and in the atmosphere. It was a gradual process, for which it is not easy to assign the exact and definite location in order of time; some placing it (with Miller, apparently) after the Carboniferous, others better (with Dawson) after the Laurentian, itself an era of immense duration.[21] But evidently it must have preceded any except the lowest forms of animal life; and hence the place it occupies in the narrative conforms in general to the known order of nature. Their emergence as signs marking off the appointed seasons, the "days" and the "years," was, as has been said, the setting up of the great world's clock, which has not varied the hundred thousandth of a second, some have claimed, in 2000 years.[22]

But we hurry on. The graphic pen-stroke that opens the fifth day's work gives us the

[21] "It is probable that the Archean era is longer than all the rest of the recorded history of the earth put together" (Le Conte, "Geology," p. 274).

[22] Mr. R. A. Proctor however says that "the resistance of the tidal wave acts as a break constantly retarding the earth's turning motion, though so slowly that fifteen hundred million years would be required to lengthen the terrestrial day by one full hour" ("The Great Pyramid," p. 209, note).

waters bringing forth abundantly,—"swarming" with living creatures. The earliest life was a long marine era, and the geologist, Le Conte, unconsciously echoes the very words of the Scripture when he says that the "early seas literally swarmed with living beings," beginning in the Cambriam,—and that 10,074 species have been found in the Silurian rocks alone. Sea life was the first main exhibition. And a mighty exhibition it was. For following close upon these Silurian species, and in fact beginning there, came the vast outburst of fishes that fill the Old Red Sandstone, or Devonian, so full.

But "the winged creature," says the narrative, was to fly "over the face" (Hebrew) of heaven. And in this same Devonian series they begin with the ephemeris—Platephemera antiqua—of five inches spread of wings, and two other species of neuroptera, expanding in the Carboniferous into a dozen other known species, one with a seven inch spread, and culminating in the Jurassic and onward, with those many kinds of monstrous winged creatures, Pterosaurs or flying lizards—some of them extending their wings twenty-five feet from tip to tip, and well-nigh darkening the face of the sky—followed at length or accompanied by the true bird with feathers—the archaeopteryx, also of the Jurassic, and by numerous species in the Cretaceous.[23]

But still another mark of this wonderful era were the great monsters of sea and land— תַּנִּינִם —the "stretched out" creatures. A singular description; and a marvellous fulfilment does science record. Huge reptiles and amphibians, in vast variety. The world offers, at the present time, of living species, not more than six species fifteen feet in length, the largest of them not longer than twenty-five; but then, from the Carboniferous through the Cretaceous periods, not less than one hundred and seventy-five known species, ranging from twenty, thirty, forty, fifty, to eighty feet in length, and one—the titanosaur of the Jurassic—a hundred feet in length and at least thirty feet in height, and possibly even this excelled by the *atlantosaurus*.[24] How the earth must have groaned with the tread of these huge and multitudinous monsters, while the face of the sky was shadowed by the screaming pterosaurs, and the waters had

[23] Sixteen species discovered in 1871 and 1872 by Marsh in New Jersey and Kansas, two of them of gigantic size. Sir John Lubbock, in 1881, adheres to the belief that "some of the footsteps on the [earlier] Triassic rocks are those of birds." "Inaugural Address to the British Association," Sept. 27, 1881.

[24] Sir J. Lubbock, "Inaugural Address," Sept. 1881.

long teemed with marine life. Could three short, bold sketches of the pen more admirably characterize the grand obvious features of the ages from the Cambrian to the Eocene?

And now the sixth day, like the third, has its double achievement. First came "the cattle, beast of the earth and creeping thing"—the popular description of the domestic animals, the larger wild beasts, and the great indefinite multitude of smaller creatures, picturesquely described as "creeping" or moving over this great globe. Why need I dwell on that magnificent fauna which followed the abrupt disappearance of the great reptiles and amphibians and marked the period of the Eocene and onward, as the well-known "*age of mammals.*" It would be a thrice-told tale to enumerate the wonderful exhibition of the Meiocene, for example, beside which the whole fauna of modern India "pales in comparison"; for there we find seven species of elephants, five of rhinoceros, four of hippopotamus, three of the horse tribe, the terrible deinotherium and their associates,—although it is only close upon the time of man's appearing that we find his faithful companions, the sheep, the ox, the goat and the dog. The characterization of the period from the reptilian to the human is striking and admirable.

And at the close of all,—according to both the records,—comes man himself, and, according to both alike, he came to "have dominion" over the beast of the earth, the fish of the sea, and the fowl of the air. In other words, from his first discovered and rudest vestiges, at the remotest periods, wherever we meet him, he is *a man*, with a capacious skull and a stalwart form, with weapons and implements, the hunter of the reindeer, mammoth, musk-sheep and woolly rhinoceros, and elsewhere, and perhaps later, buried in his skin-robe with ornaments of shells and perforated teeth, with his red war paint,[25] and use of fire, and, while living side by side with the mammoth, carving on a plate of ivory the likeness of his huge contemporary;—a man with all the essential qualities of a man, though far away from the radiating point of the race—and no doubt degraded by the far-off wanderings.

Now, in glancing back over these two records, in the book and in the rocks, which I have thus summarily sketched, one may well

---

[25] So thinks Dawson. "Nature and the Bible," p. 164. It was red oxide of iron. This occupant of the cave of Mentone was the contemporary of the cave-bear, and regarded by Lyell as "palaeolithic,"—although others express doubt, chiefly, it would seem, because of the progress indicated.

ask how it was possible with a few grand pictorial strokes so distinctly, so vividly and so intelligibly through all time, for the book to have delineated, ages ago, in consecutive order, the great procession of Nature from her inception to her consummation. How we are constrained to come at length, and to lay beside this early coherent narrative the scattered discoveries and deductions of a great multitude of acute and exploring minds, and to bring their discoveries and deductions into coherence along the unbroken line of the ancient outline sketch. And it is of no account if some minor or exceptional detail is not reported. There is no room nor reason for such things in our square-inch map.

See, then, the sources of the history of this universe as they lie in a continuous series, confirmed by all the latest research in at least the following particulars:

1. Nature and its parts had a beginning. So, certainly, science shows of all the parts; and in regard to the whole, it leads us up step by step by progressive approach and points us to the beginning of all. "The whole course and tendency of Nature so far as science now makes out," says your Professor Young, "points backward to a beginning." And he speaks not only for such men as Tait, Thompson, Clerk

Maxwell, and Helmholtz, but in the name of reason herself.

2. That all Nature is one great coherent system. On this point the latest science speaks in even more and more emphatic terms.

3. That there was once a chaotic condition in which no life existed nor was possible.

4. That the fitting up of this world was a progressive work.

5. That light was antecedent to and independent of the sun's performing its function for the earth.

6. That the earth was once sheeted with an envelope of waters, "nearly or quite universal," and the heavens with vapors.

7. That there came a time when continents and seas began to form.

8. That vegetation next appeared anterior to animal life.

9. That only at an advanced period in the earth's progress did the heavenly bodies perform for it their present functions.

10. That the early, if not earliest animal life, was an immense sea-life.

11. That winged creatures follow, strikingly conspicuous.

12. That an age of huge reptiles and amphibians—sea and land monsters,—followed or accompanied.

13. That after this came the great mammalian movement, as we call it.

14. That man was the greatest and last step of the creative work.

15. That he made his appearance with his peculiar and human faculties, lord and master of the animal world.

To appreciate the marvellous character of this account, I need not lay beside it the fragmentary hints from Babylon, the absurdities of Hindoo, Egyptian, Chaldean cosmogony, or even the utterances of Hesiod. We may turn to classic antiquity in her bloom, and see the best she could say by an Augustan poet:

> "Once, sea and earth, and sky that covers all,
> One face of nature were in all the globe,
> Which men call chaos, rude and formless mass,—
> Nothing but inert weight; discordant seeds
> Of jarring things were all together heaped.
> No sun was yielding to the world his light,
> No growing moon renewed her youthful horns,
> Nor hung the earth in circumambient air,
> Balanced by its own weight; nor did the sea
> Stretch out its arms along the distant coasts.
> Where'er was earth, was also sea and air.
> Thus faithless was the earth, pathless the wave,
> And dark the air; its own fixed form belonged to none,
> Each thing resisted each; in every part
> Cold fought with hot, and moist with dry,
> And soft with hard, the heavy with the light."

Much of all this, whether called poetry or not, it will be seen, is sheer nonsense. The sequel avoids the same confusion only by confining itself to an imaginative picture of the earth's surface and surroundings—including however an actual division of sky and earth into five zones,—closing indeed with man the "ruler of the rest." Yet man's history is in doubt,—

> "whether from seed divine
> Formed by the maker of a better world,
> Or the new earth just severed from the sky
> Retained some seed of kindred heaven, which,
> Mix'd with water from the stream, Prometheus
> Formed to the likeness of the mighty gods."

And yet before this shallow account of what is called the origin of the world saw the light, there had been for nigh fifty years beyond the Tiber, within a mile of the palace where Ovid waited on Augustus, a colony of captives in whose homes undoubtedly there lay copies of the Hebrew manuscript which more than a thousand years had been proclaiming to men the short, clear, simple story of the order of the creation—the great primal source of history.

LECTURE SECOND.

EARLY MAN.

It will be observed that nothing in the first chapter of the Pentateuch is decisive for or against the theory of evolution. No utterance therein contained informs us whether the production of all these various occupants of the earth and seas was a direct or mediate process. If there is a statement conflicting with the evolution theory in its extent, it is to be found rather in the second chapter, at the creation of woman. We need not be precipitate in dealing with the subject. The scientific objections to the theory, in its extreme form, have always seemed to me even more insuperable than the scriptural ones. It is not necessary to have spent one's life in collecting or exploring all the facts of natural history to understand the force of the reasoning employed upon these facts. It is competent for any clear-headed thinker to say whether that reasoning is sound or unsound.

One can readily admit what has long been known, the fact of very great varieties existing in any species—varieties often suddenly produced and yet permanent, as in the otter breed of sheep and the Niata cattle. But they are, so far as has yet been shown, however great their deviation, kept within such limits as not altogether to lose their normal character. Perhaps no greater range of variation is found than in the hundred and fifty races of dogs, more or less, from Spitz and poodle to bull-dog, St Bernard and Newfoundland. Yet in quality and character, however devious in detail, they are evermore unmistakably dogs.

The theory of a gradual evolution requires an infinity of time which astronomers find themselves less and less able to grant, while its common accompaniment of natural selection as the sufficient explanation has been often shown to be, in Mivart's words, "a puerile hypothesis" and encounters the obstinate facts of species like the globigerina and the terebratula caput serpentis remaining unchanged from the Cretaceous to the present time, and the lingula even from the Cambrian,[1] together with the *universal* absence of the alleged connecting links from genus to genus;

[1] St. George Mivart, "Contemporary Review," 1880, p. 37. Am. Reprint.

as it encounters, on the other hand, the startling abruptness of the entrance of many a new and multitudinous species, not accounted for by any supposed loss of intermediate strata, as in the *unbroken* geological transition from the Silurian to the Devonian, and from the Cretaceous to the Tertiary; and the theory of evolution *per saltum* also fails of showing a connecting relation and scarcely differs from a direct creation; while considered *merely* as natural unfoldings, both alike break down before the moral nature—the reason and will—which forms the huge hiatus, the impassable gulf, between the animals in their highest estate and man in his lowest. While we may patiently and candidly examine all evidence, nothing can well be more futile, it seems to me, than what Mr. Huxley was pleased to call a "demonstrative evidence,"[2] drawn from finding some six entirely distinct species of the horse tribe extending from the Orohippus of the Eocene—about the size of a fox,—to the modern horse, by assuming from certain similarities, particularly of the hoof, attended with very considerable differences, that the one certainly sprang from the other. The transition process is precisely what remains to be proved. It is like the

[2] Lecture in New York. Sept. 22, 1876.

case of finding a half-dime, a dime, a double dime, a quarter, a half-dollar and a dollar with even an identity of composition and great similarity of external formation, and declaring that therefore the dollar is "demonstrated" to have been evolved from the half-dime.

If ever the theory can be fairly shown to be a fact, we will cheerfully accept it, and adjust our difficulties to it—none of which however appear in the first chapter of Genesis. Let us be careful not to resist evidence. But thus far, "not proven" must clearly be the verdict.

Meanwhile we have in the Pentateuch a connected, though greatly abridged, account of the condition and institutions of primeval and primitive man, long the sole knowledge, but now beginning to be supplemented and confirmed by fragmentary disclosures of archæology. Let us look at this narrative and its confirmations.

(1.) What was the locality of his earliest habitation? Our narrative presents us with a first and a second point of departure for the human race—the second substantially the same with the first. What was that? No doubt indefinite confusion has been thrown over this question, in some cases perhaps not unwillingly. A class of writers have been more than ready to convert this, with all its surroundings, into a myth. And so the place has been made impossible by thrusting in among the rivers, the Nile and the Ganges or Indus, and among the countries, Ethiopia and India. One Christian writer would help out the confusion by adding to the Nile and the Ganges the fabulous "ocean-river" of the Greek classics as their common bond. For the Pishon no less than seventeen streams or bodies of water have been suggested, and for the Gihon not less than eighteen. Among them thus far we do not find included the Mississippi or the Amazon,—although we do find the Jordan and the Danube. Some would escape the whole difficulty by affirming a probable transformation of the earth's surface at the Deluge; while others simply affirm it to be an insoluble question. It must be handled cautiously.

Still it must be seen that the Biblical account of the Garden of Eden has all the traits of an exact geographical description, endeavoring to set forth the place by recognizable facts—the general region, the rivers that proceeded from that region, the countries they watered, and the productions of those countries, even to the particular quality of the gold there found, that it is "good." Now the first of these rivers is unquestionably the Euphrates, and the region of its rise is a well known and settled fact. The second, the Tigris, is almost equally beyond question, and its chief sources are within a few miles of the Euphrates—2000 paces, says Delitzsch (Comment *in loco*). The general region is thus somewhat definitely and positively *settled;* and here are the two greatest rivers of the country. Now midway between two principal sources of the Euphrates, ten miles from each, rises the third great river of the region, the modern Araxes, called by the Persians, Jichoon-ar-Ras, which Reland, Rosenmüller, Von Raumer, Kurtz—(and Delitzsch doubtfully[3]) with good reason identify with the Gihon. The old difficulty—that this river encompasses the land of Cush and that Cush must be Ethiopia,—has passed away. Modern research has found an ancient Cushite race in this very region. Gesenius was obliged unwillingly to extend Cush from Ethiopia into Arabia, and Robinson to make it the immense region reaching from "Assyria on the N. E. through Eastern Arabia into Africa." Rawlinson at length[4] showed a remarkable connec-

[3] He says of the theory which would include the Phasis, the Araxes or Oxus, among the rivers, and identify Havilah with Colchis, "It is a possibility which Kurtz and Bunsen rightly regard as relatively the most admissible"—although he finally surrenders the question as insoluble.

[4] Rawlinson, "Herodotus," i. 353.

tion between the Cushites of Ethiopia and the early inhabitants of Babylonia; Lenormant accepts it as a "proved" fact[5] that there was a race of Cushites on the lower Euphrates and Tigris, Kushites of Babylon, before the Chaldean occupants; and Maspero[6] lays it down as settled that three principle Cushite peoples established themselves around the Persian Gulf. The first, called Cossæans or Kisseans, by classic authors, settled on the mountain region that extends to the east of the Tigris; the second spread along the lower Tigris and Euphrates; the third occupied the southern regions of the Persian Gulf, which it left for the coast of the Mediterranean.[7] The first of these would occupy the land compassed by the Gihon or Araxes, and there remains but the fourth

---

[5] "Chaldean Magic," pp. 337-347.

[6] "Histoire Ancienne," p. 147.

[7] Dr. A. Wieseler (Zeitschrift für Kirklische Wissenschaft, 1882, p. 3) finds Cush in the highlands of the Caucasus north of the sources of the Euphrates and Tigris. "For this use of the term I have adduced two grounds; (1) that the Kas in Caucasus, which corresponds to Cush, (comp. also the mountains of Casius) etymologically among the Scythians according to Pliny ("Nat. Hist." vi. 17) and Bopp in J. Grimm, ("Hist. of the Ger. Lang." p. 234,) signifies a rocky mountain; and (2) that the Indian Caucasus is still called Hindu-Cush. So the clearer and obscurer expressions, Kash and Kush are interchanged with each other, a fact which can be confirmed by those Indoscythian legends."

great river to find. Many have made that fourth river Pishon, the old Phasis, now Rion, which flows from the Caucasus into the eastern end of the Black Sea. But perhaps more probable (though lacking any traceable connection of name) is the far larger and nearer stream the Kizil Irmak, or ancient Halys, the southern sources of which are on the western slope of the Karabel mountains, that separate the springs of the river from those of the Euphrates, at a spot seventy miles E. N. E. from Sivas.[8] Now, as Reland long ago showed, (followed by Rosenmüller,) the Hebrew "Hav-

[8] Chesney's "Euphrates and Tigris," i. 3. It should be added that nearly all who advocate the situation of Eden in Armenia fix upon the Phasis for the Pison, with a similarity of name indeed, but with great difficulties in regard to the smaller size and far greater distance of the stream. The transfer of a name in the lapse of ages is no impossible thing, as is seen in the name of the wilderness of Paran, which now seems to survive only in Wady Feiran at a very considerable distance from the wilderness which it once designated. Were it not for the remoteness and smaller size of the Phasis, this would have, in the similarity of the name, a claim to be considered the Pison which no other stream presents. In failing to find such a resemblance in the Halys or Kizil Irmak, which makes the doubtful point, one encounters only the same difficulty in regard to name which besets all the other suppositions, while the *fact* corresponds. So far as I am aware, Col. Chesney was the first to suggest the Halys instead of the Phasis. It is the practical suggestion of a skilful British engineer who had ex-

ilah" is, in its consonant elements, slightly transposed, the same as Colchis—the latter having the Greek termination added. Colchis lay at the eastern end of the Black Sea, extending somewhat indefinitely toward the south. It was the land of "the golden fleece" and, according to Strabo (I. 45) had great riches of "gold and silver." If we might (with Onkelos, the Jerusalem Targum, the LXX., the Vulgate, Fürst and others) identify the Hebrew *shoham* with the emerald or green beryl, and what is perhaps more doubtful (though maintained by the later Rabbins, by Bochart and Fürst) the "bdellium" [בְּדֹלָה] with the pearl, the case would be still stronger, inasmuch as Pliny, Solinus and Diodorus Siculus declare that the emerald abounded in that region and the pearl fishery is mentioned in the Periplus as existing on the coast of Colchis.[9] Round this region on the south flows the Kizil Irmak, till after a course of seven hundred miles it enters the Black Sea. In this region ancient silver mines are known to exist for a distance of two hundred miles, from Madeh to Yuzgat and perhaps Divrigi. And though in the un-

plored the general region in two successive expeditions, and has therefore some great advantages over the *speculations* of men who have never visited the country.

[9] *Ib.* i. 279, 280.

explored condition of the country now it is not easy to fix upon any considerable traces of the more precious metal, yet its existence in that region is indicated alike by early fable, ancient historians, and modern testimony.[10]

In this great plateau of Armenia, within a radius of some ninety miles, there thus rise the four great rivers of the whole region, flowing respectively to the north-east, the east, the south and the south-east, 1600, 1150, 1000 and 700 miles, all springing from the various rivulets which form the water-supply, "the river-system" (Kurtz), the system of water-courses, the collective נָהָר of the region.[11]

---

[10] *Ib.* pp. 276–9. Most of the speculations of modern German scholars on the locality of Havilah are made valueless for the sober expositor by their assumption that this narrative is a saga, and that Havilah may be sought at random in India or elsewhere,—or as Friedrich Delitzsch puts it, in Utopia. This latter writer, in accordance with his theory, would find it in that part of the Syrian desert bordering on the Euphrates and extending from the Persian Gulf northward as far as Babylon. A part of the region, he says, is at present called Ard el-hâlât, or land of downs ("Das Paradies," p. 59). It has commonly been asserted that this Havilah is necessarily identical with that of ch. x. 7, 29, xxv. 18, 1 Sam. xv. 7, 1 Chron. i. 9. For reasons to the contrary, see "Keil's Commentary" *in loco.*

[11] For the use of this word (in the plural) to designate waters (translated "floods") see Jonah ii. 3, Ps. xxiv. 2. The Hebrew had no such combination as "river-system." Thus Wetstein in Delitsch's Genesis, (and after him Fried-

We may not give special weight to the fond tradition, still cherished in the valleys of Central Armenia, that Eden extended from the northern part of the pashalik of Mosul to a point not far north of Erzeroom, to Tocat in the west and somewhat beyond lake Van in the east;[12] nor to the tradition, still living at Harpoot, that paradise was on the adjacent plain;[13] nor to the name Paradise-mountain (Edenis-Mta) that still lingers on a lofty peak in the Caucasus above the sources of the Rion.[14] But in all the learned confusion that has been cast over this subject, we can at least say that it is possible to find a local habitation for the Scripture site, somewhat clearly, by two certain landmarks—the sources of the Tigris and Euphrates—with a reasonable conformity to the description in other respects, in a tract of country (the highlands of Armenia) which, in the words of Col. Chesney, confirmed by him

---

rich Delitzsch) dwells on the necessary oriental notion of watering a garden, that it was by a multitude of little rills, countless little streams running in every direction. Indeed any other conception of the formation of four great rivers from the same נָהָר in a hilly region such as that where the Tigris and Euphrates originate is out of question.

[12] Chesney, i. p. 267.
[13] H. N. Wheeler, "Letters from Eden," pp. 15, 16.
[14] Freshfield, "Central Caucasus," p. 277.

in detail, "owing to the variety of its surface, climate and temperature, is adapted for the growth of almost every tree that is pleasant to the sight or good for food."¹⁵ And whatever difficulties of detail may attend this location fixed upon by Reland, Rosenmüller, Kurtz, Bunsen and others, it has a tangible basis, avoids all "mythical" and self-contradictory elements, meets no insuperable objections, and finds various confirmations. And somewhere in this region of Armenia eastward, perhaps on the southern slope of the Taurus, though some would prefer a somewhat more southerly site, it certainly is not unscriptural to find the home of our first parents, as well as (in this general region) of the second set of progenitors of the race. "The mention of the rivers Tigris and Euphrates," says Kurtz, "points to this [the highlands of Armenia] beyond the possibility of a doubt." And Friedrich Delitzsch who in his elaborate investigation would fix upon a region in Babylonia just north of Babylon, does so on the basis that "as to the Tigris and Euphrates no doubt is possible."¹⁶ Others (Calvin, Bochart,

---

¹⁵ Chesney's "Euphrates and Tigris," i. 270.
¹⁶ "Wo lag das Paradies," p. 11. Friedrich Delitzsch effectually demolishes what he calls "Paradise in Utopia" —i. e., all those theories which introduce impossible combinations (such as the Nile, Ganges, Indus), in a discussion

etc.) would find it still farther south, below the junction of the Tigris and Euphrates. But whether higher or lower, all sober exposition of twenty pages. But when he reaches the "Paradise in Armenia," he dispatches it in four pages, and with arguments of slender force, chiefly the difficulty of finding Cush and Havilah, and secondly of deriving the four streams from one. He shows, as others have done, that the South Babylonia Paradise is probably unsupportable, inasmuch as a very large part of the present delta has been formed even in historic times. His argument in behalf of his own theory is perhaps more ingenious than convincing.

The difficulty, dwelt upon by Delitzsch and others, of one "river" dividing into these four great rivers, is geographically and hydrostatically insuperable. It is however easily solved if by "river" in the first instance we understand water-supply, river-system, streams collectively. Delitzsch would find the garden of Eden in Babylonia between the Euphrates and Tigris where they approach each other nearest. His view of the one river divided into four is that the Euphrates is the one, and that this, supplying a canal or arm (Pallikopas) which leads from the Euphrates to the Persian Gulf, also the Shatt en-Nil, another branch which returns again into the Euphrates, and to some extent sending water through canals to the Tigris, meets the problem of the one and the four. One is compelled to feel that with all his German ingenuity and exhibition of learning, his argument labors in every direction, alike in his identification of streams, names, and to some degree countries and their productions—as when, *e. g.*, he would find the shoham in the cornelian. He has done good service in exploding the "Utopian" theory and in showing that the delta, so to call it, of the Euphrates is of more recent origin.

must fix upon the neighborhood of these streams—and according to the narrative, apparently toward their sources.

Now toward this region in general, Western Asia, or as some would say, Western Central Asia, various confirmatory indications point, for the cradle of the race. It must be admitted that it is easier to find objections than proofs in reference to any definite place. But the general region along the Tigris and Euphrates is settled by the narrative. Here in the neighboring Caucasus is found the central and highest form of the human species; radiating from around the elevated central region of Asia, says Quatrefages, we find the three fundamental types of humanity, the black man, the yellow man and the white man."[17] And Guyot has well shown how, as we recede from this general Asiatic centre in every direction, the tendency is manifest towards a more or less complete deviation from the best perfection of the human face and form;[18] Brunton in the interests of ethnology would look towards the neighborhood of the mouth of the Euphrates;[19] Friedrich Delitzsch for reasons partly geographical and largely speculative, to the re-

[17] "Natural History of Man," p. 51.
[18] "The Earth and Man."
[19] "The Bible and Science," p. 363.

gion around Babylon. So too, linguistic affinities lead us back toward this general region as the representative and radiating centre of the languages of the world. In reference to some of the languages, as, *e. g.*, the Aryan, the several lines of divergence towards the south-east, south, south-west, north-west and west are as distinct as the diverging lines of the ancient glaciers of North America. Towards western Asia—indeed towards this same region—point the great Semitic group; and if in other cases the indications are less defined they still comport with such an original home.

In western Asia seems to have been the original home of the domestic animals. Of thirty-five species of these that may be called cosmopolitan,—man's attendants,—not less than thirty-one appear to have been natives of Central Asia or Northern Africa.[20] So also of grains. The six-rowed barley of the Greeks, Romans, and Egyptians, and the Egyptian wheat, point to the great plains of Western Asia as the locality whence they came.[21] When in the Swiss lake-dwellings of the so-called Neolithic age we find two kinds of barley, three of wheat, and two of millet together with the pig, the goat and cattle,

---

[20] Southall's "Recent Origin of Man," p. 43.
[21] "British Quarterly."

these domestic animals and cultivated cereals make their first appearance *en masse,* not one by one; implying that the villagers arrived with flocks and herds and seeds. Meanwhile the earliest traceable inhabitants of Chaldea, the originators of the arrow-headed alphabet, though found on the plain, bear the name "Accadian," which means mountaineers, and their alphabet itself, in the character of its signs, indicates as the original home of the writing a more northern region with a very different fauna and flora, where the lion and the other great carnivora of the feline race were unknown, while the bear and the wolf were common animals.[22] Among the earliest traces of man in Europe we find an oyster-shell from the Red Sea at Thayngen grotto near Schaffhausen, and fragments of the *nephrite* of Asia in a paleolithic cave at Chaleux, France, connecting them all with either an Asiatic origin or relationship. And it has been observed, in the same line, that when in Europe we reach the time of bronze implements, swords, axes, spear-heads, razors, knives,—these, however widely dispersed, by their unity of design and form indicate a community of origin. And from this general locality how easy to discern the historic

[22] Lenormant, "Chaldean Magic," p. 359.

track of the migrations of the tribes to their distant homes, and, in part, to account for their line of march towards the severals points of the compass.

But in what condition was primeval man? The Scripture represents him as once in a state of moral equilibrium, a friend of God. And here the traditions of the nations, with their golden age of innocence and happiness, re-echo the statement. It belonged to the Egyptians, Chinese, Hindoos, Greeks, Persians, Thibetians, and as Lenormant remarks, " is found among all the nations of the Aryan or Japhetic races, belonging to them prior to their dispersion and being one of the points in which their traditions place them most expressly on a common basis with those of the Semitic races, with those that find expression in Genesis."[23] He calls it "one of the universal traditions." But while innocent, the Scripture consistently supposed man in a state of moral immaturity and inexperience, involving the danger and the fact of the fall.

In regard to early industrial condition, the claims of the scriptures are moderate. Some light employment among the trees that furnished his food was his earlier task, and his first clothing of the simplest kind, like the

[23] "Origines de l'Histoire, p. 58."

grass or skin coverings of the rudest tribes at present, or the skin robe of the old man of Cromagnon. Here is no nonsense about the "rivers flowing with milk and with nectar," while "honey dripped from the trees." He was to dress and keep the garden. His sons are found in the simplest modes of rural life. keeping flocks of the smaller animals, sheep and goats, and tilling the soil. The arts in their higher form came in only in the seventh generation, with Jabal, Jubal and Tubal Cain —of which more hereafter. Meanwhile notice the sobriety and consistency of the narrative.

As to his intellectual condition there is an equally noteworthy consistency. It is sufficiently manifest that a human being, however mature in size and strength, entering on life without experience, would require some immediate and preternatural knowledge as a substitute for experience; otherwise he would be like the new-born infant in capacity to care for himself, and the day of his creation might easily have been the day of his dissolution. His very faculty of sight would be misleading, and all his muscular powers unmanageable. While therefore the scripture consistently and necessarily ascribes to him a precocious intelligence and some linguistic development, as exhibited in fitly giving names to the animal world and in recognizing the contrast of his own solitude, there is a clear intimation of his practical inexperience in his being directed *by his Creator* to make the clothing of skins, and perhaps also in the absence of all surprise in Eve's listening to the speech of one in the form of a serpent.

The scripture thus makes a fully consistent picture,—of one in the balance of the moral nature, with Augustine's "posse peccare et posse non peccare," yet without the formed character which will make the security of the ransomed; and, intellectually, of one entirely destitute of the industrial arts and scientific attainments, but with a mental capacity full-grown. Nor is there in my judgment anything to discredit this Biblical account in the various researches in the history of the race, but the contrary. It has become customary enough to assume with Lubbock and others, as an axiom, that man started as a low savage, even if not an animal, yet little above the animals. That he actually started not indeed with the arts, but with a high capacity for their rapid development, may appear in the sequel.

It is a singular process of reasoning to take the distant outcasts of the race, tribes that wandered far away from the native home and had been subjected to all the depressing and degrading influences attendant, and to insist that *they* are representatives of that native home. History shows that there is not only such a thing as progress, but such a thing as degradation. And modern researches are more and more pointing us back to a centre of early light, intellectual and moral, and bringing to distinct recognition the fact that the greater the distance in space, if not in time, from the central seat, as a rule, the greater the depression. How unequal has the human race, in its highest attainments, shown itself, unless preserved by a supernatural grace subduing its own innate seeds of corruption and destruction, to maintain its high attainments, and how certainly has come the descent and fall! The old empires all are startling illustrations. It remains to be shown, if it can be shown, that aside from the presence of a supernatural revelation and preserving influence, there is such a thing as *permanent* progress of the human race. All history thus far goes to indicate that if the human mind is an active thing it may also be a destructive thing, and in the long run human depravity overtakes and overthrows human culture, and worries down human refinement. Every new expansion of archaeological inquiry seems tending to give new emphasis to this solemn lesson of all history.

It is one of the latest and growing theories of philologists to regard the old polytheisms of Egypt, Greece, and India as the corruptions of an older monotheism. And a great orientalist informs us that the one thing which a a comparative study of religions places in the clearest light, is the inevitable decay to which religion is exposed.[24] It has become one of the astounding revelations of modern times to see how far, far back of all consecutive history many of the arts and forms of civilization stand out before us, as it were full-grown. The great cities of Babylonia in ruins reveal a surprising early development. The stupendous works of Egypt burst upon us without a known history. Her whole sculpture is a decadence. We gaze upon the green diorite statue of Cephrenes (or Shafra), and we say it is certainly a portrait,—and how wonderfully superior to the formal statuary of later times. We gaze upon the still older wooden image of the village *beled* or sheikh, so wonderfully life-like, and we say here is something far better yet. And when we look upon the two older ones of Nefert and Ra-hotep from May-

---

[24] Max Müller, "Chips from a German Workshop." Preface xxii.

doom, "the oldest statues in the world," we say these are the best of all. Equally remarkable that oldest picture in the world, of the pasturing geese from the tomb of Nefermat, as compared with later Egyptian paintings, so-called.

So again we look at the early development of the Aryan races in comparative proximity to their early home, the Sanscrit speaking race, the Persians, and the Greeks, and we cannot fail to contrast their condition with that of their kindred, the long wandering Celtic and other tribes that were driven to the distant west. We witness the Caffre language apparently descending into the Hottentot, and that still further falling into the Bushman. We find men, e. g., the Tasmanians, living on an island without the knowledge of canoes that must have brought them thither.[25] Or take a still more remarkable and recent instance. In 1866, Dr. W. A. Marten made a journey to Honan in China, on purpose to visit a Jewish colony, one of many supposed to have existed formerly in the empire. This at Honan has long been known to the Christian world, having been discovered by Father Ricci in the 17th century, and claiming to have entered China as early as the Dynasty of Han. Dr.

---

[25] Lubbock's "Prehistoric Times," p. 450.

Marten found a remnant of 3000 to 4000 completely demoralized and even unjudaized. A solitary stone marked the place of their synagogue, on which an inscription commemorated its erection, about A. D. 1183. They had copies of the law and the prophets, of which no man was able to read one word. With a rabbi, the father of one of Dr. Marten's visitors, had perished, forty years before, the last vestige of acquaintance with the sacred tongue. They have no knowledge of their tribe pedigree, keep no register, and now never assemble in a congregation. They remember the names of the feasts of Tabernacles and of unleavened bread as practised by a former generation, and have lately abandoned circumcision. One of them had lately became a Buddhist priest, another had a heathen wife. The living generation had pulled down their synagogue and sold its stones and timber to obtain relief for their bodily wants, and the large tablet that once adorned its entrance, bearing in gilded Chinese characters the name "Israel," now belongs to a Mohammedan mosque. The only distinctive mark that is left them is the custom of picking the sinews out of the flesh they eat—commemorative of Jacob's conflict with the angel.[26]

[26] "The Chinese," pp. 295-7. Harpers, 1881.

The Veddas of Ceylon, now savages of the most debased type, are degenerate descendants of the tribe who brought Aryan civilization to Hindustan. "More than half their words," says Max Müller, are corruptions of the Sanscrit; "they may possibly prove in language, if not in blood, the distant cousins of Plato, Goethe and Newton."[27]

Now, with such specific illustrations before us, and with our eyes upon the singular collapses of great nations, as in Egypt, Greece and Italy, where printing and especially Christianity had not found their way, or the latter had lost its power, how can we for an instant maintain that savagism was necessarily the primitive, rather than derivative state of man. I anticipate that more and more the process of research may indicate that in fact it was not so, and that the standard of ancient humanity is no more to be sought in the caves of Neanderthal, Liège, Mentone, or Furfooz, than that of modern civilization in the Bushman, the Australian, the Terra del Fuegian or the Sioux Indian. Physical degradation also accompanies the moral and intellectual.[28]

What now were the early institutions of man? Here we may glory in our Pentateuch

---

[27] Geike's "Hours with the Bible," i. p. 165.
[28] On this subject see Argyll's "Primeval Man," p. 155

The second chapter of Genesis has well been called the most momentous of records. In its announcement of man's early institutions—its provision for his fullest destiny—it shines out on this dark world like the flash of light through chaos. There is nothing like it. Two great institutions, founded upon his deepest wants and nearest relationships, were to have been the guaranty of his well-being, and are now the hope of his future.

The first was that of marriage and the family, as defined in that great original law of monogamy, which in its first perfect form was issued in paradise. Was there ever an utterance like it, except in the New Testament exemplification of it? Woman taken from the side of man to indicate identity, intimacy, sympathy, dependence, to call for tenderness, shelter, protection—the two to be bound together as one, in an indissoluble bond, above that which binds any and all other earthly relationships—"one flesh," "bone of my bone and flesh of my flesh." Herein lies the cradle of the home, and the empire of woman. When was ever such a picture drawn except in that same holy book—as when the apostle finds in the relation of Christ and his church, in the supreme self-sacrifice on the one hand and the profound love and devotion on the other, an unfolding of the symbol of marriage. It is a sublime, a divine, conception (Eph. v. 25-33). How on the one hand do the true marriages that are "made in heaven," and on the other the polygamies and the divorces that are made in hell, flash their sacred or their lurid light over the grandeur of God's primal institution for man. And it will be observed that when polygamy creeps into history, it is first as the doing of the Cainite race, and, in the patriarchal line, as the offspring either of a want of faith in God, or of fraud, and as the germ of family trouble. And it is also to be observed how futile must be all attempts to raise or maintain the position of woman except on that divine and primeval basis. All history shows that the race was made for wedlock. It also shows that, whether in or out of wedlock, woman is and must be from her constitution the weaker and the dependent, and in a fight for ascendency the weaker must go to the wall. It shows, too, if it shows anything, how vain is the hope of a radical improvement of the human condition by external arrangements that leave the human spirit unchanged, full of its selfishness, malignity and brutality. A swine in a garden is none the less a swine. And when we look upon the awful separations and horrible relations that human sinfulness creates so continually between the nearest of relatives and friends, sown in guilt and reaped in crime, we are brought back to the obvious fact that the only adequate remedy for the wrongs of woman is a return to the divine ideal of the true relationship. No crusade of blind complaints and reproaches will eradicate the cause of complaint. No scramble for man's functions —whereby she becomes not masculine but mannish—will make the woman content. No acts of legislation will carry happiness into a discordant home, or protect the victim from the destroyer. But just so far as the great law of paradise is restored and realized, just so far will come—as has been coming—all needed outward reform, founded on the inner spirit that alone will make the law a life and a fact. All observation and all history lend their sanction to this divine original institution. In the formation of the woman we find the greatest apparent scriptural obstacle to the theory of evolution. Mr. T. L. Brunton admits this to be so; "If we are to take the words of the Bible as an accurate account of the creation of woman, I do not see how we are to reconcile it with the doctrine of evolution."[29] The details of the narrative at this point are

[29] Brunton's "Bible and Science," p. 353.

so brief and so obscure that it is easy for any man to ask questions that no man can answer. We cannot say with certainty that the צֵלָע was a rib. The word elsewhere designates more nearly a *side*, as of a mountain, the tabernacle, an altar, the heavens, as a door, a side chamber, the side of a man;—perhaps in two passages (I Kings vi. 15-16; vii. 3) the beams of a building, in no case clearly the human rib. But if not this, what then? Was it some portion of the frame originally added for the purpose of being removed? We can only say that it was one of similar portions remaining, (צְלָעֹת plural.) Some[30] have gone so far as to accept the theory of the Talmud, the Targums and Maimonedes, of an original androgyous man, afterwards *separated* into man and woman— a construction which forces the narrative out of shape; for God took the צֵלָע and "*made* it into a woman." If we understand this to be in all respects a literal and objective statement, we still have, remarkably sustained from the first, the law that now prevails through all life—that, as Huxley would say, the living protoplasm comes from living protoplean—life from previous life, the woman comes from the man.

Nor can we with Brunton call this "a par-

[30] Lenormant, apparently, "Origines," p. 58.

able." For the account bears as fully the aspect of a narrative as any other portion of the Pentateuch, and to admit such a deviation would throw us upon an ocean of uncertainties. Delitzsch[31] approaches nearer an admissible hypothesis when he intimates that it may be a "symbolical" narrative.

But there is perhaps a possible solution for those who seek it, growing out of the recorded fact that the man was cast into a "deep sleep" (תַּרְדֵּמָה) before the formation of the woman. And we may possibly compare the similar state of תַּרְדֵּמָה in the fifteenth chapter of Genesis (v. 12), in which Abram received the communications of God, and apparently had the vision of the pillar of smoke and flame passing between the divided victims and symbolizing the covenant of God with him. It may be thought possible to understand that Adam's sleep in like manner continued and the following transaction was the vision in that sleep whereby God signified to him the indissoluble union with the wife. But even in this case there remains the fact asserted not only here, but in 1 Tim. ii. 13, that "Adam was first formed, then Eve." And in accepting the fact we accept no greater difficulty than the evolutionist here encounters, nor so great; for in

---

[31] "O. T. His." p. 23.

God's agency, deliberately establishing the relations of the sexes, we have an intelligent plan and cause, and a rational end in view, from the beginning; whereas that great unchanged, perpetual and substantially equal relation of sex that runs through not only the human race but all the countless races of the earth, is one of the problems before which any theory of evolution that excludes a grand preliminary plan and a mighty governing power, only betrays its helplessness and puerility. It is one of the insoluble problems for any form of development hypothesis that excludes the final cause and the First Cause.

The other signal institution of primeval man, which met him apparently at his origin, was that institution which lies at the foundation of all outer worship of God and all organized beneficence towards man, the bulwark of society, the supplement of the home, the universal refiner and civilizer, the guaranty of social order and friendly relationship, the institution whereby all other human institutions are preserved and made effective—the seventh sacred day. It is difficult to see any propriety in understanding the narrative of its establishment as a prolepsis, or any cogency in the reasons rendered for thus forcing the narrative. It clearly is recorded as a part of the preparation of the world for man. Man's whole nature, physical, intellectual, social, moral and spiritual, has been proved over and over to coincide with the Saviour's declaration, "the Sabbath was made for man." The whole record is consistent with itself. For besides the indications of the week usually recounted from the Pentateuch, as repeatedly occurring in the narrative of the flood, the time of circumcision, the weeks or heptades of Jacob's courtship, the seven days of Joseph's mourning, we find the complete or sacred number in God's assurance to Cain of a "sevenfold vengeance," as well as in Lamech's "seventy-and-sevenfold," and even incorporated into the Hebrew language in the term for *swearing*, which is to "seven oneself." It is hard even to believe that when Cain and Abel came with their sacrifices, apparently at the same time, and that time "the end of days," this end of days was other than the sacred seventh day. That the nations in their dispersion and moral deterioration should have lost the observance, as very likely had the Hebrews during the slavery of Egypt, was to have been expected. And yet there are indications enough of the wide diffusion of this hebdomadal division of time to connect themselves in a very striking way with the primeval appointment. Bunsen affirms a seven days division for astrological purposes in China to be of proved antiquity;[32] it was known to the ancestors of the Hindoos;[33] and would seem to have been known in ancient Egypt, as well as a period of ten days. How extensively it can be traced among the northern nations of Europe is a field for further inquiry. But at Athens the sections of Prytanes, apparently as early as the time of Cleisthenes, held office seven days at a time; and one of the very latest results of oriental research is the positive statement by Geo. Smith, Sayce and others, that from a very early period—before the migration of Abram—the Accadians of Babylonia and Chaldea had the seven-day week and the sacred Sabbath,[34]

[32] "Egypt's Place in History," iii. p. 290.
[33] Dr. Burgess in "Bibliotheca Sacra," Oct. 1858.
[34] Mr. Richard A. Proctor, who has devoted a large amount of space, in his recent volume on the "Great Pyramid," to the advocacy of the theory that week originated from halving the lunation and then halving that half, naively remarks, after his prolonged discussion, that "a more careful study of her [the moon's] motions suggests the division of the lunar month into six periods of five days each rather than into four periods of seven days each." If he had said that not only a "careful study" but *perpetual observation* would sooner suggest the one first than the second, he would have been quite safe. See the "Great Pyramid," p. 272.

wherein no work should be done. The attempt to explain this wide-spread arrangement as a subdivision of a lunar month is not sustained by the planetary names given to the days; and meets the obvious difficulty that the week is not an aliquot part of a lunation—the latter being twenty-nine and a half days, of which by far the nearest proximate division would be the very close division of ten-day periods, which also prevailed in Egypt.[35]

And the institution of that form of worship which took the shape of sacrifice, after the fall, "at the end of days," stands singularly confirmed in its survival through all times and almost all races of the earth. So that it is of little moment whether we view it as a direct divine appointment or an instinctive impulse of the human soul; for the amazing tenacity with which it has clung to the race in all its wanderings, bears testimony to its inherent necessity to primeval fallen man, and confirms its early origin.

The narrative of the first sin too, has not only a consistency that grows on the contemplation, but offers the only solution of the dim traditions of the distant past. It has been not uncommon to question the fitness of the pro-

---

[35] Sayce, "Chaldean Genesis," pp. 89, 308. George Smith, "Chaldean Discoveries," p. 12.

hibition as a test of obedience, as though out
of keeping with the magnitude of the occasion.
But a moment's reflection shows that not only
could the principle of a genuine obedience be
tested as well in that mode as any other, but,
what is more important, that some such method was the only one in keeping with the
circumstances of the narrative, and further yet,
the only method practicable in those simplest
conditions of early life. All the complicated
relations of advanced civilization and even of
society were wanting. Here were two persons
in a garden of nature. Fraud, theft, adultery,
arson, robbery, were impossible, murder as
yet inconceivable, all overt acts of cruelty, if
not impossible, yet without a possible motive.
What other form of test could or can well be
devised than just such as that adopted, standing
thus related to their *actual life and condition.*
To a profounder reflection it carries on its face
the stamp of verisimilitude, and those more
striking devices which the objection would require, would, in their inconsistency, brand the
narrative as untrue. And while in some aspects mystery must hang over any speculation
on the modes of the first human sin, our narrative offers perhaps all the help that can be
given when it traces the source of the seduction to an *outer* influence, distinctly explained

in the New Testament,[36] as "that old serpent which is called the devil and Satan," and when it couples with the persuasions of the appetite the specious inducement of a higher good—"ye shall be as gods"—and a pressure applied to the more emotional of the pair. And while the real agent is thus identified with Satan, I see—in accordance with a narrative which described all *as it appeared*—no fair mode of escaping from the recognition of the actual objective appearance of a serpent, chosen for the reason suggested in the narrative, the subtlety of the movement that comes and goes so stealthily and so unexpectedly, and the association thereby awakened. The one grave objection, that this is the concession of a miraculous transaction for the purpose of deception, is perhaps sufficiently answered by saying that to them it was no miracle,—for there was no adequate knowledge of a settled course of nature,—but an ordinary phenomenon.

I stand the more firmly by this view, from the striking confirmation which is found in the ancient and wide-spread traditions of the east, pointing definitely to precisely such a transaction. We not only find the sacred tree that gave immortality—the Indian Kalpanksham, the Persian Hom, the Arab

---

[36] Rev. xii. 9; xx. 2; John viii. 44.

Tuba, the Greek Lotus, the tree in the coffin at Warka, and Babylon named "the place of the tree of life;"[37] we also find the ruin of the race connected with the eating from a tree, in the Edda of the north, in the Zendavesta, and in the legend of Thibet, and a deceiver also appears, who is in some cases the serpent.[38] Indeed the serpent figures largely in traditions, in Egypt, Chaldea, Persia, Phenicia and elsewhere, as the enemy of the gods.

The confirmation becomes more definite and singular still. We find not only a Babylonian cylinder of the 9th century B. C., showing the sacred tree with attendant figures and eagle-headed guardians, and another cylinder showing the sacred tree with "attendant Cherubim;" but we find another early Babylonian cylinder with sacred tree showing fruit, a seated human figure on each side, each with a hand extended towards it, and a serpent behind the one whose hand is nearest to the fruit;[39] a vase from Cyprus of the 6th or 7th century B. C., (now in the Metropolitan Museum of N. Y.) from the branches of which hang two large clusters of fruit, while a great

[37] Geike, "Hours with the Bible," pp. 116–7.
[38] *Ib.* p. 119.
[39] Smith's "Chaldaische Genesis," ed. Friedrich Delitzsch, pp. 98, 87.

serpent approaches and prepares to seize one of them with his mouth; a famous sarcophagus in the Capitoline Museum shows, near Titan, son of Iapetus, who performs his work as moulder or designer, a man and woman standing nude at the foot of a tree from which the man makes the gesture of gathering the fruit; a bas-relief laid in the wall of the garden of Villa Albani at Rome presents the same group, with a serpent twined around the trunk of the tree under the shade of which the two mortals stand.[40] All these are the distant echoes of the scripture record, drawing their significance from that simple story of which the same sacred volume offers also the solution. "In all antiquity the serpent was the symbol of cunning, baseness and seduction."[41]

For the promise of the tempter was fulfilled like those of later tempters,

> "That palter with us in a double sense;
>   That keep the word of promise to our ears,
>   And break it to our hope."

They did indeed "know good and evil," the one as lost, and the other as fatally found. And thus, too, emerges the force and symbolism of the doom pronounced upon the real

---

[40] Lenormant, "Origines," pp. 92-4.
[41] Tuch, "Genesis," p. 84.

tempter—for against him was it aimed. It involved no change in the animal, the reptile, whose change from an erect to a prone position and motion would have involved a change in every muscle, bone, process and organ of the body,—a re-creation,—but it was a curse in symbolic form. A serpent's form thou hast assumed, a serpent's doom and destiny shall be thine; thy career shall be that of a wretched crawler and dirt eater, inflicting with thy poison a dangerous, and possibly fatal, wound upon the woman's seed, but receiving in turn a crushing blow from the seed of the woman, and especially from that chosen seed who was revealed "that he might destroy the works of the devil," and who in token of that ascendency and dominion so often ejected Satan's agents from the demoniacs of Palestine.

Ejected now from that home of innocence and from the tree of life, that sacramental tree,—which like the sacred bread and wine could symbolize but not give immortal life, and of which the eating were now a profanation till man stands again by its side on the banks of the river of life,—he began his experience of that threatened death of which all history bears witness, and of which the essential fact was never so well expressed as by Augustine when he said, "death of the body is the separation of the body from the soul, but death of the soul is separation of the soul from God." For in this fruitful central germ is all sin and all resultant woe. Then and thus all the moral faculties work abnormally, falsely, and therefore, wretchedly.

And so that death showed itself first in the sense of shame; then in the shrinking from God's presence; then in crimination, the one of the other and of God; unfolding still further in the fearful utterance that announced all the pain, anxiety and woe that gather over woman's lot in connection with her offspring, and with the frequent tyranny of the husband taking the place of the normal and loving protection and dependence, and in the perversion of man's toil from its normal pleasantness to be a drudgery, wearing and uncertain in the process, and bitterly disappointing in its best earthly hopes and fruits, and ending in the physical decease which, though not the primary gravamen of the threatened death, is yet its sad and fitting symbol. And how soon all this horror for the man and the woman and the world culminated in the first fratricide. How the history of the murderer down through all time was delineated in that titanic and terrible figure, which represents the earth as opening her mouth to receive the blood of the victim and hurling back from that open mouth a curse upon the criminal. And in the remorse and terror that weighed him down and chased him through the land of "wandering," haunted by the presence of God and the threatening spectral hand of man, and that made him build his fenced city or stronghold, like some mediæval robber's castle, we read by anticipation the vivid pictures of the masters of tragedy and romance, in some Macbeth or Sykes, or the facts of actual occurrence as in the Knapps and Crowninshields of real life. Meanwhile in the trials and sorrows that have embittered the social life of the race, in the burdens and anxieties that have poisoned their labor, in the crimes and woes that have filled the earth and assailed the heavens with their cries and groans, and in the thick and heavy clouds that have hung over human prospects further back than the dawnings of human history, we read the substantial verity of the sweeping curse pronounced upon the progenitors of our race— the ancient anathema travelling downward through the centuries, till it meets one who comes up "alone with dyed garments," but "travelling in the greatness of his strength, speaking in righteousness and mighty to save."

LECTURE THIRD.

THE EARLY ARTS.

A NOTEWORTHY feature of our advanced civilization is the unconsciousness with which we inherit a vast mass of things—utensils, usages and methods—the discovery or invention of each one of which has been a great stride in human life and achievement. We justly glory over our modern inventions, many of which, such as photographic, electric, and steam apparatus, began in the application of the simplest principles, at first in a modest way, and which waited almost to our day for that first rude application. It is with profound surprise that we walk through some collection of ancient relics, as in the museum at Naples, and see there anticipated so many things, such as dentist's implements and the like, which, we had supposed, belonged only to modern times; or, that in still more ancient collections, like that of the Boulak Museum in Cairo, we look upon a modern fish-hook, the children's dolls and playthings, the paraphernalia of ladies' toilets, or the superb jewelry of an ancient queen. But far more remarkable are the commoner inheritances from the past, so identified with our daily life that we never think of their origination. Yet those were bold men who first ventured upon many an article of our food, and to the last degree ingenious men who first devised a multitude of processes connected with its preparation. The grinding of grain, the use of leaven, and a thousand things connected with the sustenance of life, whence came they? So with the commonest appliances; a nail, a screw, a pulley, a lamp, a pair of scissors, a chair, a table, a kettle, a chimney, the forging of metals, the making of glass, were in some sense grander inventions than the steam engine and its contemporaries, because they enter so closely into all the daily round and comfort of living of all men.

It is interesting to see how the oldest mention or implication of many of the great conveniences and processes of common life is found in the sacred record. And here the narrative is not only self-consistent, but is abundantly sustained by the remotest investigations of the latest time.

The brevity of an ancient narrative often reveals only by suggestion or implication. The first clear indication of primeval implements is to be found in the coats of skins. For, the sewing of the fig-leaves, as we gather from the use of the word תָּפַר and its equivalents תָּפֵל and טָפַל, was not necessarily more than tying them or making them in any way adhere together. But the preparation of the skins involves, to say no more, the use of cutting instruments. And it is noticeable that here the suggestion is by implication ascribed to the Creator, in the statement that "the Lord God did make coats of skins and clothed them." Simple as is the flint knife—simplest of all effective instruments—the first invention of it *for the hour of need* might well be ascribed to a God-given sagacity. And its invention may equally well be traced to the origin of the human race, inasmuch as all, even the rudest tribes of men in all ages, have been found in possession of sharp implements of flint or other hard stone. They occur no less among the relics of palæolithic races and Swiss lake-dwellers of Western Europe than among the North American Indians and their predecessors the mound-builders, and in the lowest stratum at Hissarlik, two unknown ages earlier than the Troy of Homer; and in Egypt deep below the ground in a well near Cairo have been found flakes of flint evidently fashioned by the hand of man. With them enter the first faint traces of human presence on the face of the earth. The stone age has but recently passed away from among the Esquimaux, and it prevailed over the world till the inventions of the higher races have entered. The fact is suggestive, and might possibly be explained as the result of the same permanent necessities and constant ingenuity, or more easily, when we see the same style of chipping away the flint all over the world, as the result of an earliest, common inheritance. Thus there is, it is said, a noticeably close resemblance between the palæolithic implements in the post-glacial terraces of Trenton, N. J., and those of the gravel beds of northern France and southern England.

But we are led to another still more remarkable inquiry, that concerning the early use of fire, as perhaps involved in the narrative. To say nothing of the tilling of the earth by Cain, even though perhaps not for the cereals but for roots and garden vegetables, as naturally if not necessarily supplemented by the use of fire, yet the sacrifice of Abel, "the firstlings of the flock and of their fat," involves, unless the offering stands isolated from all else of the kind in the Bible and the history of the nations, a consumption by fire. And it is noticeable that even in the previous narrative an apparently archaic word, properly designating the "licking" of fire occurs in the phrase "the flame of a sword," לַהַט הַחֶרֶב (Gen. iii. 24). The long-matured and skilful application of fire is of course involved in the forging processes of Tubal Cain at a later period, and the first distinct mention is found in connection with the burnt offerings of Noah. A moment's reflection, while it shows the momentousness of the discovery, shows also the singular improbability of that discovery being made by any being however intelligent anterior to all knowledge or conception of its uses, and much more the improbability that it should have become the common possession of all the remotest races, unless by some such community of inheritance and therefore early origin. Yet no race on the earth has been found destitute of it, although it is asserted (by Lubbock and others) that some races have not the power to produce it. Lubbock, after referring to some three alleged exceptions, is constrained to say, "It cannot be satisfactorily proved that there is at present or has been in historical times any race of men entirely ignorant of fire. It is at least certain that as far back as the earliest Swiss lake-dwellings fire was well known in

Europe."¹ This is not all. While it has been common to admit that in the so-called palæolithic period of Europe, fire was probably known, but "there is no evidence of it,"² it seems that this last statement can hardly be made. Indeed a sharp distinction between palæolithic and neolithic man is becoming for various reasons more difficult to maintain. It will hardly answer to draw the line on the ground of progress attained; for that begs the question at issue.³ The palæontological test founded on the presence or disappearance of extinct animals seems on some accounts fairest.

[1] "Prehistoric Times," p. 560.
[2] Winchell, "Preadamite Man," p. 415.
[3] Archibald Geike, though earnestly maintaining a long lapse of time in Britain for the palæolithic period ("Ice Age," p. 504) and a sharp dividing line between its relics and those of the neolithic age (p. 496), yet informs us in his later work ("Geology," 1882, p. 903) that the nature or shape of the implement cannot be always a satisfactory proof of antiquity. "We must judge of it by the circumstances under which it is found. The student may profitably consult Dr. Arthur Mitchell's *Past in the Present* for the warnings it contains as to the danger of deciding upon the antiquity of an implement merely from its rudeness." And Dr. J. W. Dawson remarks ("Origin of the World," 1877, p. 278) that "Wilson, Southall, and other writers have accumulated so many examples of this that I think the distinction of Palæolithic and Neolithic ages must now be given up by all investigators who possess ordinary judgment."

This as proposed by Lartet makes (for France) the oldest period of the cave-men the time of the cave-bear, the next of the mammoth and woolly rhinoceros, then that of the reindeer, and last of the aurochs. Lubbock so far agrees as to make the earliest period that of the cave-bear, mammoth and rhinoceros.[4] But at Massat ashes and charcoal were found not only in connection with the bones of the bear and other animals, but with a likeness of the cave-bear himself drawn upon a stone.[5] So at Aurignac, which Lartet regards as "reaching back to the highest antiquity of man," in conjunction with the bear, mammoth, and rhinoceros were found marks of fire.[6] It has been found in large quantities in the valley of Vèzére,[7] which however may be later. Connect with these facts that ancient legend concerning Prometheus, which declares the greatness of the boon, the source, and the strangeness of its procurement, and all these indications concur with the supposition of its communication to the first family. In the same direction lies the statement of the Phenician cosmogony

---

[4] "Prehistoric Times," p. 2.
[5] Southall, "Recent Origin of Men," p. 208. Quatrefages, "Human Species," p. 146.
[6] Lubbock, *Ib.* p. 320.
[7] Quatrefages, "Human Species," p. 320, 145.

which reckons as descendants of Genos and Genea (Cain and Caina), three brothers, Light, Fire and Flame.[8]

In the same direction lies the brief announcement concerning the occupations of Cain and Abel, the one a cultivator of the soil, the other a raiser of the small cattle, sheep and goats (צאן). The two simplest of all occupations, our narrative informs us, began thus early. It is in keeping with Livingstone's observation after his long experience among the African tribes, that it is out of the question for human beings to maintain life by dependence simply on the unaided products of nature. The origin of these employments lies beyond the verge of all other history. The Scripture account thoroughly accords with all we know of early life. The Swiss Lake-dwellers had their various grains and domestic animals. Several writers have endeavored to show that the men of the stone age in France and Suabia had their domestic animals, horses and reindeer. It is, perhaps, an open question. But it would seem to be no question that agriculture and cattle breeding marked the earliest progress in Europe beyond the life of hunting and fishing.

We would not venture far in speculating—

[8] Lenormant, "Les Origines," p. 20°.

though almost compelled to raise the inquiry—what utensils are necessarily supposed in this early keeping of goats, as always, for their milk. But we are reminded at once how ancient and well-nigh universal has been some kind of pottery, however rude. It abundantly marks the sites of "all ancient habitations," as well as the chief resorts of the Indian tribes, the mound-builders' settlements, the Celtic towns, and the old Lake-dwellings.[9] It was found in the valley of Massat with the remains of fire and of the cave-bear; at Nabrigas where the bear's skull-bone was pierced by an arrow, and at Vergisson in connection with four extinct species of animals.

Furthermore, we are told that Cain built a city. The word, by its origin and frequent early use, designates no more than an enclosure for defensive purposes, a wall or ditch, either or both, surrounding a dwelling or cluster of dwellings. We may understand a rude structure far simpler and less elaborate than the mound-builders' strongholds on the Miami and in Northern Ohio, and in size at most a hamlet or encampment rather than a modern town. For we may remember that in early Judah there were one hundred and twenty-four "cities," and in Canaan thirty-one royal

---

[9] Lubbock, "Prehistoric Times," p. 237.

"cities," that even the city of David was originally but a citadel on Zion. Homer's Troy, at least the fortified part, the city proper, appears to have been but a hill fortress with an area scarcely two hundred feet by three hundred, not half so large as the fortified hilltop of the old Egyptian miners in Wady Magarah.[10] The city (עִיר) in Isaiah i. 8, is apparently but a watch-tower. We may therefore imagine simply an enbankment or stockade, within which the terror-stricken criminal endeavored to quell his fears and secure his safety, as in later days the Pequot chief Sassacus retreated within his stronghold to shelter himself from the avenger of blood.

The next clear indications of progress that occur in the sacred record, are found in a remarkable outburst in a singularly gifted family, Lamech and his sons, Jubal, Jabal and Tubal Cain. It occurs naturally enough after the lapse of some generations, and in the Cainite line,—the men of this world. The development is so surprising that some have endeavored (like Buttmann) to remit it wholly into the region of myths, and to regard the three as gods, early worshipped by the Hebrews; others (as Ewald) would find three great classes into which the civilization of that age

---

[10] About 660 by 260 feet.

was divided; and Lenormant would regard them as ethnic personifications of the great human races, Tubal standing for the Tibareni and the Chalybes. It is difficult to read such statements into the text. But the progress recorded is very great; it follows in the line of him who founded the first city or permanent place of habitation, and is attended with circumstances of luxury, sensuality, boastfulness and ferocity which give a striking air of verisimilitude to this brief opening into the oldest civilization of the human race.

In the possession of Jabal we find tents and cattle,—these last no longer the smaller animals, the sheep and goats of Abel's time, but the larger cattle also, constituting together already, as in later times, a great oriental fortune. The tents in which they dwelt to care for their flocks and herds set before us, as already mature, no doubt, the art of spinning and weaving the goats'-hair cloth which from time immemorial has formed the black oriental tent, and, by natural inference, of converting the wool of the sheep into clothing. And the picture of life thus given would correspond in good measure to the life of Abraham and Isaac in after times, when they had their home in Palestine, rich in flocks and herds, with more or less settled places of abode, yet moving about with facility as necessity or convenience might require. Historically the arts of spinning and weaving reach back beyond all other records. The neolithic men of the Swiss lakes present us with cloth for clothing and nets for fishing.

Jubal appears as the ancestor of those who handle the stringed and wind instruments. And it is remarkable how far back in antiquity we encounter musical instruments, and that too in great variety. We cannot find their origin, but they meet us in the full stream. The Assyrian sculptures, being mostly hunting and battle scenes, give us more meagre disclosures, although we find the harp at their feasts, and when the king goes forth from Susa to receive his prisoners, he does it to the sound of the harp and the double pipe. But Egypt furnishes both the oldest and most abundant exhibition. "Paintings on the tombs of the earliest times"[11] exhibit their fondness for instrumental music, which blossomed out into a singular variety of instruments. They had their drums, their tambourines of three kinds, clappers, cymbals and trumpets, flutes of reed, wood, bone and ivory, single pipes with three and with four holes, double pipes, and stringed instruments of much greater variety in form

[11] Wilkinson's "Ancient Egyptians," i. pp. 83, 126.

and number of strings than are in modern use. There were guitars of two or three different shapes, lyres of diverse forms, standing and portable, harps of still greater variety, some of them in shape almost like the Irish harp, with thirteen different numbers of strings varying from four to twenty-two. Thus "the harp and the organ," that is, the stringed and the wind instruments of music, antedate all other history than that of the Pentateuch.

Among the far-off tribes of the Stone Age, as it is called, we find less of artistic turn in any form, and for reasons which I shall dwell upon more in the sequel. Bones pierced with holes for whistles are the sole representatives that we find of the musical tendency. The incipient artistic turn showed itself more in other forms—in the pictures of the cave-bear, of the reindeer, of two reindeers fighting, of a fish, of the mammoth "etched upon his own ivory" so as to be perfectly recognizable, all of the earliest, rudest times. What other arts, implements, and habits of these times are indicated, whether rites of burial, religious observances and the like—I will not discuss, it not being essential to my purpose, and the facts as yet too uncertain.

But at this point let me enter two important caveats, (1) that the non-discovery of certain objects, especially in scattered caves, is no proof that they did not exist, and (2) that the condition of things in these remote places is no safe criterion even of the state of society from which they might have been detached. Unsettled tribes, and even distant colonists, leave behind far more than they carry.

Take a striking instance. The Plymouth settlers in 1620 brought with them no means of fishing, neither seines nor hooks, and for eighteen months they suffered greatly for the want of them.[12] For three or four years (till March 1623 or 1624) they had no cattle, and then but four were imported. In May 1627, they had but one cow and two goats for each thirteen persons; and the first recorded introduction of sheep, five in number, was in 1630. Horses must have been many years later. And most singular of all, though glass windows were introduced into England in 1180, yet 460 years later Edward Winslow was writing to George Morton in England, "Bring paper and linseed oil for your windows."[13] Oiled paper to keep out the cold of a New England winter! They brought with them, of course, almost no jewelry, no paintings

[12] Young's "Chronicles of the Pilgrims," p. 171.
[13] *Ib.* p. 237.

or works of art, no organ nor instruments of music—and the like. Now about the year 1852 I happened to be in Plymouth, Massachusetts, when in the construction of a drain or sewer some bones of those who died in the first year of the settlement were dug up. Suppose that the objects found with them, or that could have been found for many years afterwards, had been taken as a criterion of the state of the arts and the condition of society in England whence they had come so directly across the ocean—how illogical and false the inferences.

The third of this family group, Tubal Cain, was "an instructor of every artificer in brass and iron," or as most modern scholars render it, substantially, a "forger of all tools (or implements,) of brass and iron." Here we strike the origin of metallurgy, especially the working of brass—or rather bronze or copper—and iron. The bronze or copper comes first in the order of mention, as it appears to have come first in the order of use. Indeed it is noteworthy that early researches bring us very little of pure copper; but the main supply of metallic implements is of bronze, a compound of copper and tin. Copper is comparatively fusible and malleable, and is found in combinations much more manageable than iron, and is far more abundant in the region of Armenia and the neighboring countries. It is still a product of Armenia, being exported in large quantities, a characteristic product of Cyprus, to which it gives name, and is found in the region of Sinai. Almost as far back as we can trace anything, we can trace the mining of copper. In the neighborhood of the copper slag-heaps at Wady Magarah, is inscribed on the cliff the oldest known carved name of a monarch, Snefru of Egypt, who wrought these mines before the Great Pyramid was built. And the oldest description of the mining process is that graphic picture in the twenty-eighth chapter of Job—

> "Surely there is a vein for silver
> And a place for gold where they fine it,
> Iron is taken out of the earth,
> And brass is molten out of the stone," etc.

So early was copper and bronze forged in the East that we cannot discern the preliminary stages. In this country we can trace apparently the transition period with the old mound builders. Until recently, copper was found in those ancient works only in its native state, as it had been brought from the mines of Lake Superior and shaped into hatchets or other forms by hammering,—the process being betrayed by the lamination. The art of fusing it was supposed not to have been attained. But we seem of late to have found the transition. For in Wisconsin there have lately been discovered certain copper implements (chisels) which are declared by practical founders to have been cast in a mould.[14] This stage of transition has not been recognized in the old world — unless at Hissarlik. Schliemann found there in the two strata older than his Troy, pins of copper much harder than that of commerce, which, it is conjectured, may owe its hardness to a natural alloy of rhodium, such as was ascertained to have caused a similar hardness in the weapons of the Peruvian Incas and in certain weapons discovered at Lake Superior.[15] In what he considers the Troy stratum the metal was bronze. The proportion of tin varied from four to nearly nine per cent. Bronze was one of the abundant alloys of ancient Cyprus. Bronzes are found at Babylon and Nineveh, in which the proportion of tin is ten and eleven per cent., but in a bell fourteen—indicating a skilful adjustment. So in the bronzes of Mycenæ

---

[14] "Historical Collections of Wisconsin," vol. vii., p. 101.
[15] Schliemann's "Ilios," p. 251, 738.

a much larger proportion of tin occurs in the armor than in the domestic utensils, some of which are almost pure copper. Loftus found what he calls brass ornaments (more likely bronze) in the mounds of Erech (Warka), and at tell Sifr a singular variety and quantity of copper articles in a copper-smith's shop, where even the dross from his castings indicated his forge near at hand. The date was pronounced by Sir Henry Rawlinson to be about 1500 B. C. Bronze abounds in Egypt from the earliest times, a cast cylinder bearing the name of Pepi of the sixth dynasty. This would carry us still further back —according to Mariette 2200 years, according to Brugsch 1700, and according to Birch more than 500. In other words, however far back of the confines of all recorded history except this Pentateuch we go, we encounter bronze coming down from beyond in comparative abundance as one of the very earliest forms of metallurgy, and in the very regions to which it is assigned, and where it is still to be found. But the tin with which it is alloyed furnishes at the same time indications of an enterprise and traffic quite noteworthy, inasmuch as the nearest known points of its production are Burmah in Asia, Bohemia, Sardinia, Siberia and Spain in Europe. Capt.

Burton however, is said to have found it in Midian.

Of iron, too, Tubal Cain was the forger. Here again is a congruity to known circumstances. Iron is one of the metals of Armenia. There are mines of it in Kurdistan,—the mountains of Tyari, and the valley of Berwari. But its use among the nations generally was later and scantier than that of copper and bronze. There is no trace of it in prehistoric Troy and Mycenæ; nor in Cyprus. Among the Accadians it is said to have been a precious metal. Og, king of Bashan, had his bed of iron. It was the latest metal of prehistoric man in Europe. Only in the region of Asia referred to does it appear early to any extent. At Nimroud in one room Layard found scale armor of iron, almost decomposed with rust, but enough left to fill two or three baskets. A perfect helmet was also found, and other armor of iron and of copper, and iron inlaid with copper,—helmets of various shapes, that fell to pieces as soon as exposed. He also found iron swords, daggers, shields, spear and arrow heads, the head of a hatchet, and specimens of bronze cast over iron. These bring us nearest in place if not in time to Tubal Cain. For except in one case, neither iron nor steel is actually met with among the antiquities of Egypt; although steel is thought to be clearly delineated in the pictures. That one exception is quite remarkable. It was communicated to me by Dr. Grant Bey of Cairo, first orally, then in writing, as follows: "In 1837 Mr. Hill, in the employ of Col. Vyse, discovered a fragment of iron in an inner point near the mouth of the southern air channel of the great pyramid. It was sent to the British Museum with three certificates signed by Hill, Perring, Andrews and Mash, to the effect that the iron had been left in the point between two stones during the building of the pyramid, and could not have been inserted afterward. Col. Vyse also thought he perceived the remains of an iron fastening in the chamber containing the sideboard[16] in the great temple of Abou Simbel."

But this remarkable family had other accomplishments. For from the mouth of Lamech we hear the earliest poetry in the world's history, the triple Semitic distich in which he

---

[16] Mr. Birch, in the last edition of Wilkinson, mentions a few other small objects of iron, of which the age is more undefined: a falchion blade under a sphinx at Karnac, the blade of an adze, and iron wires sustaining the core of a broken bronze statue—the latter of the age of the Ramessids. (Vol. ii. p. 251.)

commemorates his murderous exploit and his
ferocious spirit to his two wives.

> "Adah and Zillah, hear my voice,
> Wives of Lamech, listen to my speech:
> For I have slain a man for my wound,
> And a young man for my hurt:
> If Cain shall be avenged seven-fold,
> Truly Lamech seventy and seven-fold."

It has been conjectured by many to have been prompted by his son's invention of metallic weapons; and as it was a sword-song, so was it a blood-song, an utterance of "titanic insolence" and ferocity. It well illustrates how polygamy and cruelty, lust and fierceness go hand in hand, and how the antediluvian chivalry that could name its women, "Shade" and "Beauty" and "Pleasantness," and sing to them poetic strains, could summon them to witness its ruthless revenge. In it lay already the expression of the spirit that soon filled the world with violence, and called imperatively for that later edict of God, "Whoso sheddeth man's blood, by man shall his blood be shed." Its temper suggests the later epic hero, "acer, impiger, iracundus," and the awful butchery, which, when one reflects for a moment, is seen to reign through even so famous a poem as the Iliad. In its outer form this is the simplest of poetry. For the poetic form may consist in a balancing of movement, which is measure; of sound, which is rhyme and sometimes also alliteration; or a balancing of thoughts antithetically, synthetically or synonymously, as here. Since poetry, too, antedates all history, since it stands allied to music, and so often, as in the Egyptian song of the Pentaur, it is the voicing of daring personal exploits, so here, in connection with this simplest fragment, we have all the conditions of historic verisimilitude for the origin of this incipient Odyssey. Here ends the catalogue of antediluvian art with a noteworthy silence. Not a word of painting, which had practically no existence in Moses' day,[17] nor of sculpture, nor of architecture, or any of the sights that would have impressed the senses of a dweller in Babylon or Nineveh.

[17] "We may say it is only by some abuse of terms that we can speak of *Egyptian painting* at all. No people have spread more color upon stone and wood than the Egyptians, none have had a more true instinct for color harmony; but yet they never attempted to express by the gradation of tone, by the juxtaposition or superposition of tints, the real aspects of the surfaces which present themselves to our eyes, aspects which are unceasingly modified by the amount of light or shadow, by distance and the state of the atmosphere. They used not the least glimmering of what we call chiaroscuro or of aerial perspective." Perrot and Chipiez, "Hist. of Art in Ancient Egypt," ii. p. 331.

And from this early scene of worldly development, but of profligacy and violence, which explains so much of subsequent history, we turn with pleasure to that revival in the house of Seth which apparently furnishes the clue to the "sons of God" before the flood.

The next stage of art indicated in the history is in many ways remarkable. It is made supposable only by the condition of things already described, the progress previously recorded. I refer to the construction of the ark. Now, the essential facts concerning the deluge and the rescue of one pious family from destruction I take it to be settled, if any thing historical or traditional can be settled, by the joint testimony of the human race. They seem to have been branded into the memory of the human family in all parts of the world. I will not weary you with even a summary recital of this traditional knowledge, which has been so often set in array, and which comes from Europe, Asia, Africa, America, and the islands of the ocean.[16] It is inexplicable, except on two suppositions, the substantial unity of these races, with this one great central knowledge, so far at least as to have descended from one contemporaneous stock, and the stupendous na-

[16] A good survey of them is found in Delitzsch's Genesis.

ture of the historic fact which in all their wanderings and their elevation or degradation they never could shake off from their recollection. I may add a third noticeable consideration, that when we take all these various traditions and sift from them their palpable absurdities and their local colorings, we can frame from them all a narrative that lies side by side with this sober and consistent Bible history. The substance of the universal story, when thus sifted, is this: a wicked world destroyed by a flood for its wickedness; a righteous man and his family, together with pairs of animals, preserved in an ark; the ark resting on a mountain; birds sent out to ascertain the condition of the earth; an altar built and sacrifices offered. These details are sometimes much abridged, and as often greatly expanded. The birds in the Chaldean legend of Berosus go three times. In some accounts the dove, the vulture and the raven figure; in Michuacan their place is taken by the raven and the humming-bird. The vedas associate with Manu seven other holy sages, and the traditions even of the Fiji Islands give the number of the saved as eight. Not to dwell on these and other traits of resemblance or difference, the point I have in view is the construction of the ark—a very remarkable record. It supposes a skill and resources which can be accounted for only by the facts already related, this early and extraordinary development handed down from father to son, and increasing all the more rapidly by reason of longevity, till Noah could carry out effectively the Divine instructions. See, however, the sobriety and verisimilitude of the narrative, which, granting the fundamental fact, in all its details of time and circumstance conforms to the exigencies, to an extent which of itself might almost fill the hour of this lecture. It assigns indeed a long time of expectation and of preparation, understood by one great body of commentators to be the one hundred and twenty years of Genesis vi. It was an enormous undertaking, demanding all the cutting instruments and metallic implements already invented. Observe the material, as congruous to the region as was the shittim or acacia wood of the tabernacle to the region of Sinai. The "gopher" wood of the ark is admitted to be pitch-wood, therefore light and comparatively easy of working. Lexicographers, from the similarity of the consonant elements, incline to suggest specifically the cypress. Now the cypress abounds throughout Asia Minor, and Freshfield[19] mentions the cypress and the fir as con-

[19] Freshfield's "Caucasus," pp. 230, 253, 254, 275, 322.

stituting a prominent part of the forests far up in the mountains of Caucasus. It grows to the height of one hundred and twenty feet. Nothing could be more suitable. The pine also abounds in these regions. The immense pine forests on the sources of the Rion or Phasis are among the few distinct statements of Freshfield; while Thielmann mentions the pines that half conceal the ravines of the Kura on the eastern slope, and the timber that is floated down the Koissu river to the Caspian sea. The cypress or the pine would have furnished the pitch for the caulking; or if we suppose the pitch to be bitumen—as it probably was not—we are reminded of the extensive petroleum works now carried on at Buku on the Caspian, and of the bitumen springs still flowing at Is on the Euphrates. And the olive tree of which the dove brought a fresh-plucked leaf, grows also in Armenia, and is found on the south side of Mount Ararat at its foot. But the most remarkable, and equally consistent thing, is the architecture of the building; a ship with three successive cabins divided into compartments and "light to [the distance of] a cubit above" or from above, which permits us to conceive of a row of openings under the eaves, high above the range of the waters, for light and ventilation. The ark is not launched, observe, but built on dry land—possibly on some height where the pine or cypress grew, and the waters may have "risen fifteen cubits" before it floated—whence it is gradually raised and "lifted," till it "walked (הָלַךְ) on the face of the waters." But let us observe more carefully its remarkable dimensions. For while the Chaldean legend of Berosus gives us the impossible length of five furlongs and the breadth of two, and even according to the Babylonian tablet, if we may trust the figures, long given as doubtful, the size would be—reckoning the Egyptian cubit of 20.7 inches[20]—1035 in length and 103½ feet each in breadth and *height*. The last of these dimensions—to say nothing of the length—shows the wildness of the statement. But by the same standard the dimensions given in the Pentateuch would be 517 feet in length by 86¼ width and 51¾ in height. Now the largest vessel of modern times, built by the nation that is mistress of the seas, after the most approved standard of naval architecture, was the Great Eastern. The interval of time between that first recorded vessel and this of the present generation is at least more than

---

[20] Such is the result of measurements according to Gen. Sir Henry James. Notes on the "Great Pyramid," pp. 9 seq.

4000 years. But we reach this extraordinary result, that the width of the ark was just 3¼ feet more than that of the Great Eastern, and its height 6¼ feet less—while its length, being 162 feet less, would tell yet further for its strength and safety as a seaworthy craft.

The manufacture of wine is the next recorded fact of progress. This again is far the oldest mention of a process, that of making and using fermented drinks, which is nearly if not absolutely universal. And inasmuch as Noah the husbandman "planted a vineyard," the extent and plan of the planting would render it probable that the practice was older than Noah. It is, however, not every region of the earth that offers the vine for that purpose. A great variety of fermented drinks have existed, such as at least seven kinds of beer, made from malt, maize, millet, milk, cava, rice, rye, and several kinds of wine, as they are called, made from the apple, pear, sugar cane, from the agave in a large part of Asia, and from the palm far more extensively than from the vine, as in Chili, India, the Pacific Isles and all of Africa. But in Armenia none of these resorts were called for. Its fertile soil, abounding in other fruits, yields an abundant supply of grapes.[21] So also does the whole neighbor-

[21] Chesney, "Euphrates and Tigris," i. p. 97.

ing region of Georgia, and Thielmann found excellent wine among the valleys of the Caucasus.[22] The earliest record of the wine manufacture thus refers it to its legitimate surroundings. The wine of Armenia and the neighboring regions is said to be still as unfortunate in its influences as in the days of Noah.

The most noteworthy account of any early architectural enterprise is found in the tower of Babel. This again is localized in its appropriate place, the region of Shinar or Babylonia. There seems to be in the writer's mind a clear reminiscence of Egypt, when he speaks of substitutes for "stone" and "mortar." The immense structures of Egypt were of limestone and sandstone, joined by a mortar that has not lost its binding power with the lapse of ages. But had the writer implied a building of kiln-burnt bricks in Egypt, he would have intimated that of which no trace is to be found in Egypt till Roman times. There are indeed a few specimens of such ancient brick in Egypt, but so few that for a long time their existence was positively denied. The old Egyptian bricks are all of sun-dried clay mixed with straw. Nor is such a cement as the sacred writer ascribes to this tower to

[22] "Caucasus," i. pp. 88, 234.

be found in Egypt, nor, so far as I am aware, in any region but one.²³ But in this region of Babylonia we meet all the circumstances. In the fountains at Kerkuk, Apcheron and other places, one just outside the walls at Nimroud, are abundant supplies of bitumen,²⁴ which, when used as a cement, sometimes becomes harder than the bricks it binds. Here too has come down the use of bricks "burnt to a burning," (Hebrew), so hard that thousands of them show the name of Nebuchadnezzar as distinct as if burnt yesterday. Here also is that remarkable tower, Birs Nimroud, rebuilt by Nebuchadnezzar on the site of a more ancient unfinished building supposed to be the temple of Belus, and believed by some (*e. g.*, Schrader) to stand on the spot where Babel was begun. But whatever its history, the ruin, Birs Nimroud, composed so largely of burnt brick laid in bitumen, commemorates the mode of construction peculiar to Babylonia. Indeed we can ascend almost to the date of this tower of Babel. For we have but to cross the Euphrates to the ruins of Mugheir—Ur of the Chaldees—to find in the basement of its temple this combina-

---

²³ At Warka (Erech) a partial use of bitumem was made with sun-dried bricks.

²⁴ Layard, "Babylon and Nineveh," p. 202.

tion in its most primitive form. "The burnt bricks are of a small size and inferior quality, laid in bitumen, facing a solid mass of sun-dried brick and forming a solid wall outside of it, ten feet in thickness. Writing of an antique cast appears on it, and the supposed date is 2300 B. C., a little earlier than the time commonly assigned to the building of the tower of Babel."[25]

We gain no further information or intimation of the advances in art, or in the art of living, till we reach, by a long stride, the time of Abraham, although this is more than a thousand years anterior to any other authentic history. In his biography all is quite general till we find him in Egypt. Still as he comes from Haran, but yet more remarkably in Egypt and again in Palestine, we light abruptly upon the institution of domestic slavery, first in written history. He returned from Egypt with man-servants and maid-servants, and was afterwards able from his own retainers to equip a band of three hundred and eighteen armed men. We plunge here into the midst of that institution that has so filled the history of Africa. What advances, so-called, in the condition of society are involved in this fact, can be best understood from the monuments of

[25] Smith's "Dictionary of the Bible," i. p. 222.

Egypt, which exhibit such a remarkable and complicated state of civilization as nothing else could have satisfactorily demonstrated. The Theban paintings show us slaves, both white and black, in numbers, the latter even holding the dish with hand reversed, as so often at the present day.[26] They were employed within doors and without, in every mode of ministry to the grandeur and luxury of their masters. The pyramids bear perpetual witness that enforced labor existed in Egypt long before the time of Abraham, while the old Accadian code of Babylonia even legislated on the treatment of slaves.[27] So also the institution of the harem, largely filled with foreign women, in accordance with the narrative of Sarah, was early in full operation in Egypt.[28]

But of the early use of that animal so indispensable in Egypt, the camel—which was one of Pharaoh's presents to Abraham, but neither then nor later was delineated on the monuments,—we should know nothing otherwise than in this history, but for the corroborative bones which Hekekian Bey found in his excavations in the delta.[29] And the remarkable absence of this animal from all delineations

---

[26] Wilkinson, "Ancient Egyptians." i. p. 141.
[27] Lenormant, "Chaldean Magic," p. 383.
[28] Wilkinson, ii. p. 224.
[29] Lyell's "Antiquity of Man," p. 36.

on the monuments is possibly to be explained from their association with the afterwards hated Hyksos, who may have brought them from Asia, where their name originated, and who were probably in power in Abraham's time.

It was when the patriarch went up out of Egypt, that for the first time we read of a man's being "rich in silver and gold," as he was. In no other country do we so early find evidence of gold in such abundance, and of such skill in its manufacture. The gold found in Assyria and Babylonia is later in date and less in amount. Small and scanty gold and silver ornaments occur at Mughier and Warka in Chaldea. The gold of Cyprus is still later. The treasures at Troy were of the Homeric city, as is supposed, the previous strata yielding to Schliemann but three primitive gold rings, an electrum brooch, and no silver, and the lowest stratum only one small silver brooch and one gilt copper knife. But Egypt seems to have abounded in gold from the earliest times, earlier perhaps than in silver. The gold mines of Ethiopia have within a few years been brought to light in the Bisháree desert, eighteen days' journey south-east of Kom Ombos on the Nile. Here are deep excavations in the quartz rock, and ruins of miners' huts which, however, may date only from the time of the Caliphs. But no traveller up the Nile will have failed to see in the tombs of the twelfth dynasty at Beni Hassan—where the fluted Doric columns antedate by one or two thousand years those of Greece—the picture of the whole process of washing the ore, fusing the metal with the help of the blow-pipe, making it into ornaments, weighing it in scales peculiar to this use, together with the various operations of the goldsmith. But this, though older far than the Exodus, is not the earliest indication. "The same mode of washing and working it is figured on monuments of the fourth dynasty,"[30] and Mr. Birch informs us, possibly in too sweeping terms, that the nobles of that dynasty had each his own gold-worker as well as glass-blower, potter, tailor, baker and butler, his dancer, harpist and singer.[31] Any one who has seen but a part of the Egyptian jewelry that is scattered in the museums of the world, and especially the superb collection in the Boulak Museum, largely from the tomb of queen Ah-hotep, the mother of Ahmes, will need no commendation of the Egyptian jeweler's skill, even to the art of imitating the emerald, amethyst and lapis lazuli in glass.

[30] Wilkinson, ii. p. 139.
[31] Birch, "History of Egypt," p. 45.

Nefert of Snefru's time wears her necklace of rubies and emeralds. And the delicate cutting of hard stones, and even the cutting upon a glass bead the name of Amun-m-het of the 12th (or 18th) dynasty, explain where the Hebrews could have learned the art of engraving the twelve precious stones of the High Priest's breast-plate with the names of the tribes of Israel.[32] The ear-rings and bracelets sent to the bride of Isaac are the oldest written mention of the practice that is older than all other history, as is proved by the second stratum of Hissarlik and the sculptures and relics of Nineveh, and older even than this most ancient record, as is now known from the monuments of Egypt.

Here too we find the earliest mention of money transactions, and of their method. For Abimelech pays Abraham a thousand of silver[33] — a transaction more distinctly ex-

---

[32] Exodus xxviii. 15-21. "Under the first Theban empire the Egyptians practiced the cutting of amethysts, cornelians, garnets, jasper, lapis lazuli, green and white feld-spar, obsidian, serpentine, steatite, rock crystal, red quartz, sardonyx, etc. We do not know whether these early workmen employed the lapidary's wheel, but we may safely say that they produced some of the finest works of the kind which are known to us." "History of Art, in Ancient Egypt," Perrot and Chipiez. London, 1883, ii. p. 288.

[33] Gen. xx. 16, xxiii. 16.

plained subsequently, when Abraham buys the field and cave of Machpelah for four hundred *shekels* of silver, which, it is added, "he weighed to Ephron, current money with the merchant." These transactions bring out three points; (1) that in ancient times silver appears to have been the money metal, gold being reserved more for ornament; (2) that for a long period still money was not coined and stamped, but weighed—the Lydians being among the first to use coin, and that perhaps a thousand years afterward; (3) that even then the merchant, (סֹחֵר) the *travelling* tradesman was at his business of exchange. Later, in the history of Joseph, we encounter a whole caravan of traders on their way to Egypt with various commodities there in demand—spicery, balm and myrrh, to which they add on the journey the youthful slave. Of these commodities, the first two, the צֳרִי and the נְכֹאת, Ebers thinks he has found the very names in the Egyptian *tal* and *nekpat*[34] in close proximity, in the laboratory at Edfu.

The business-like method of Abraham in his traffic conforms to the careful reckonings so abundant in Egypt, and to the existence of a hundred Chaldean tablets filled with business

[34] Ebers, "Ægypten und die Bücher Moses," p. 290.

contracts, both before and after the time of Abraham.[35]

To the same volume we are indebted for our oldest written knowledge of the contrast between the elaborate civilization of the Nile, with its butlers and bakers and feastings, its irrigation, its grain trade, its leavened bread, its fine linen and dyed cloths, its embalming of the dead, its defensive strongholds and chariots and armies, on the one hand; and the simpler life, partly tent-life of Palestine, with its unleavened bread, its wells, pastures and flocks, its earthen furnaces, its skin bottles, its donkeys for burdens, its warlike mountain tribes and its degraded wickedness by the Dead Sea; and also the intermediate civilization of rural Mesopotamia, where the camel and the kine predominated in the flocks and herds, where though town life prevailed, the daughter repaired to the well with the pitcher on her shoulder, where there were teraphim, and labor-wages, and marriage contracts and wedding feasts, where the bride set forth with her household stuff, and the family were accustomed to " send her away with songs, with tabret and with harp."

So dependent indeed have we been upon these ancient records for all that is consistent

---

[35] Tompkins, "Times of Abraham," p. 36.

and coherent in our notions of this earlier state of the race, that the mere omission of any circumstance in this narrative has left a blank in history, ordinarily not to be supplied. It is a noticeable illustration that glass, whether from the difficulty of its manufacture or its extreme fragility, or from not belonging to their condition of life in Egypt or perhaps from being of far less utility than the stronger and cheaper pottery, seems not to have found its way among the Hebrews, and is never mentioned in these old historic books, nor found in the ruins of Palestine. And perhaps the simple omission was the occasion of the belief prevalent till recently, that glass was unknown, until it was accidentally discovered by some travelling Phenicians. I remember two otherwise intelligent Scotch clergymen in Rome, who still advocated this exploded notion, one of whom concluded his argument by saying, "You'll find no glass about Solomon's temple." And yet not only are objects of glass somewhat common among Egyptian relics, but the process of its manufacture into bottles is delineated in the tombs of Beni Hassan, and it is admitted to have been older than the great Pyramid; while such was the skill displayed in its manufacture, that not only was it made into artificial precious stones, but figures were wrought into glass in such wise that the pattern of the surface passed in right lines through the substance, and often so minutely exact that it could be made out only by the use of a lens.

And thus it is that many a hiatus in our knowledge comes from the reserve of this ancient book. And while many a perplexity is cleared up by its solitary voice, many others remain unsolved for want of those few words, or it may be the one word, that it does not speak. Vainly do we sometimes wish, "O that the word had been spoken." What light it might so easily have cast on a multitude of now difficult if not insoluble problems. For we might address that ancient author not with possible guesses once put to an exhumed and shrivelled corpse, but to a once seen and living witness,

> "And hast thou walked about—how strange a story—
>   In Thebes's streets three thousand years ago,
> When the Memnonium was in all its glory
>   And time had not begun to overthrow
> Those temples, palaces and piles stupendous?"

But though that witness must have been an attendant at the dazzling court of the great Rameses, no less than of the infatuated Menephtha, the Sphinx itself could not be more reticent of that mighty but boastful name, though cut so deep on half the monuments of Egypt. For what had Moses in common with Rameses? And why should he commemorate that useless name? In his imperishable record the serene lawgiver will hand down that tyrant's name neither to the fame he so intensely coveted, nor to the infamy he deserved. In all the compass of history there cannot be found a more singular case of reticence.

LECTURE FOURTH.

THE EARLY CONSANGUINITIES.

THE books of Moses, as well as the remainder of the Scriptures, seem to assert and assume the unity of the race, and their common origin. This lies not alone in the statement, that Eve was called by Adam the "mother of all living," but also in the uniform tracing of all branches and members of the human family to the one ancestry; in the assumption that the one fall affected in its consequences all the race as the offspring of Adam; and that the redemption was and is for that *one* lost race.

The methods and tendencies of scientific thought have in one respect singularly changed the aspect of this whole question within a generation. It is like one of the marvels of modern magic. Forty years ago we were obliged by laborious inductions and a wide range of observations and historical researches to show the *possibility*—then vehemently and sturdily denied—that races so diverse could have come from a common ancestry. Now on the other side, this labor is taken off our hands by the general concession, rather the vigorous assertion, of the same type of thinkers and reasoners, that anything and all things living may have descended from precisely the same kind of living germ,—not to speak of what lies still further back. It is, when we consider its celerity, certainly one of the most amazing flank-movements, and stupendous revolutions in the history of thought.

But as it may be doubted not only whether this theory has been proved, but whether it ever will or can be proved, we do not find ourselves absolved from the necessity of glancing, however briefly, at the lines of human consanguinity from the beginning of the race.

Without resorting to any evolutionary hypothesis, we may allude independently to the indications *first*, that the tribe of men *might* have descended from one pair. This ground was well canvassed, in the main, long ago. It was well shown that the physical differences now existing are no insuperable objection. These were found to be in accordance with well-known facts of wider range. Before the researches of Darwin had been given to the public, so high an authority as

Dr. Carpenter had announced as a well settled fact of observation that among the domesticated races of quadrupeds the characters most susceptible of variation are, *stature, general conformation of the body, conformation of the skull, quantity, texture and color of the hairy covering, physical character* as shown in the increase of intelligence and disappearance of some of the instinctive propensities. These comprise summarily the whole catalogue of diversities found in the human species.

In regard to the human race it has been shown abundantly and historically (1) that each of the external differences often ceases to be characteristic. Thus the black color is found not only in individuals, as the black Jews of Portugal, but in tribes, as the Bicharis on the Red Sea, whose hair and character are perfectly Semitic; and the white color in the brutalized descendants of certain exiled Irish of Ulster whose features are almost of the African type.[1] "There are negroes," says Quatrefages, "whose prognathism is no more marked than in whites, and whites in whom it is very pronounced;" the quality of the hair not being an invariable mark, nor the shape of the section of the hair—whether

[1] Cabell, "Unity of Mankind," p. 98.

oval, circular, or cylindrical—a characteristic; while other distinctive qualities of races often shade into each other. Indeed Quatrefages has abundantly shown that the limits of variation in animals of the same species are even greater than in man between the white and the negro taken as extremes, and they include color, anatomical character and external form, even to the modifications of the head.[2] (2) It has been shown that we can frequently trace the history of great physical changes, as in the Magyar of Hungary, unquestionably of the old Turanian or Tartar stock, whose residence for a thousand years in the fertile plains of Southern Europe, and consequent changes of habits therewith, have also changed the pyramidal skull into an elliptical one, and obliterated every physical trace of their Tartar features; the Turks of Europe and Western Asia modifying from the Central-Asia toward the European type; and the physical degradation and transformation wrought by even two centuries of hardship and want in Sligo and northern Mayo in Ireland.[3] (3) It also is found that often the linguistic affinity is strongest where the physical resemblance is slightest, and weakest

---

[2] Quatrefages, "Human Species," p. 2.
[3] Cabell, "Unity of Mankind," p. 99.

where this is strongest. An instance of the former kind is found in the relation of the Malayo-Polynesian and American races, and of the latter kind in that of the Chinese and Mongolian races. These fundamental points have been abundantly proved. If it be objected that the appearance of the negro is too far back in history to allow time for the *establishment* of such decided changes, the negro appearing, it has been said, as early as the sixth dynasty in Egypt, the reply is obvious and easy, that changes are often rapid and become permanent at once, especially where the same influences continue; as the Ancon breed of sheep sprang from a single male in Massachusetts in 1791, and the Mauchamp sheep in France in 1828, the hornless oxen of Paraguay from a single male in 1770, and the Niata cattle of South America which are of comparatively recent origin, but permanent. So the African race, once differentiated, might easily become permanent—especially as the conditions remain. But Quatrefages declares that "the true negro did not exist in Europe during the quaternary epoch." No fossil skull belongs to the African or Melanesia type.[4]

[4] "Human Species," p. 292. The statement that "we see negroes on the monuments in the Sixth Dynasty"

The objection arising from the dispersion of the race in primitive times across wide expanses of ocean, has been abundantly answered by reference to known facts. Lyell, for example, cites cases of island savages having drifted in their canoes from Wateoo to Otaheite, 550 miles, from Ancorso to Samar, 800 miles, from Anaa, one of the Coral Isles, to uninhabited islands, 600 miles, and from Ulea to one of the Coral Isles, 1500 miles—

(Southall, "Recent Origin," p. 26) is not quite accurate. We do not *see* them depicted on the monuments till the eighteenth dynasty. The first mention of *Nahsi* or negroes is found in an inscription at San by one Una, an officer of Pepi of the Sixth Dynasty. He records, among other things, his having levied an army of *Nahsi* from Aruret and other lands of Ethiopia. The inscription in full is given in the "Records of the Past," vol. ii., translated by S. Birch. The rendering "negroes" is accepted also by Brugsch, ("History of Egypt," i. p. 119). Mr. Birch, however, in his notes on Wilkinson's "Ancient Egyptians" (London 1878) remarks (vol. i. p. 261) "the Blacks were generally called *Nahsi* or revolters." This definition naturally raises the question how far the color is matter of inference, by reason of the provinces being Ethiopian. The reign of Pepi was long subsequent to the beginning of Egyptian history. Some 767 years are assigned by Birch in his history to the first *three* dynasties, and about 1000 years to the first six dynasties. This allows a long time for race changes. Indeed there is no absurdity in the suggestion that race tendencies might have been transmitted from before the Deluge, by the marriages of Noah's sons.

far enough to have gone from some parts of Africa to South America or from Spain to the Azores, and thence to North America.[5] Indeed it seems now conceded that all the Polynesians, from the Sandwich Islands to New Zealand, from the Tonga Islands to Easter Island, belong to the same race.[6] In many cases their traditions commemorate the ancient migrations.[7] How the communication even with America could be and in part actually was established has been abundantly indicated by Quatrefages,[8] first in the northwest across Behring's Straits, divided midway by the St. Lawrence Islands, or farther south from Kamschatka to Alaska by the Aleutian Islands, or even further south where the "current of Tessan" has frequently cast abandoned junks on the coast of California; also directly across the main ocean—if not over the Pacific from China, of which there seems to be evidence,[9] yet certainly and repeatedly from Europe—the Scandinavian appearing to have landed on the eastern coast of North America between Greenland and Long Island as many as five times from the year 886 to the year 1007, beginning with Erick the Red and end-

---

[5] Lyell's "Geology," Eleventh Ed. ii. 471-2.
[6] Quatrefages, "Origin of Human Species," p. 188.
[7] Ib. 192-8.   [8] Ib. 199 etc.   [9] Ib. 204-7.

ing with Thorfinn. So abundant and so marked have been these evidences of migration over the land and *the sea* that Sir Charles Lyell early made, and left permanently on record in his latest (eleventh) edition, this remarkable utterance: "Were the whole of mankind now cut off, with the exception of one family, inhabiting the old or the new continent, or Australia, or even some coral islet of the Pacific, we might expect their descendants, though they should never become more enlightened than the Australians, the South Sea Islanders or the Esquimaux, to spread in the course of ages over the whole earth, diffused partly by the tendency of the population to increase in a limited district beyond the means of subsistence, and partly by the accidental drifting of canoes by tides and currents to distant shores."[10]

The objection arising from the number and diversity of languages—reckoned at some 900 or more—has been met in part by the success already achieved in tracing the connection of certain tongues widely dispersed, as the Aryan from India through the west of Europe, to one common stock or family, and some of these families to a still higher connection; and the answer has been supplemented by

[10] Lyell's "Geology," ii. 474.

the express views of many of the highest linguistic authorities, as Müller and others, that there is nothing in the present aspect of the various languages of the earth to militate against the common origin of the nations.

And if it be still objected that granting the possibility of an original unity of speech, the time supposed to have elapsed is insufficient to explain the vast changes; the effectual answer has been made, viz., that the rapidity of linguistic changes varies immensely with the circumstances and conditions of life, whether under the existence of a written and diffused literature, as for the last few centuries of modern Europe, fixing its form, or in a region where there is permanence of residence and institutions, with settled and centralizing domestic relations, as in ancient Egypt and Palestine,—under both these conditions language becomes fixed and remains long unchanged. But in a country and a race undergoing great changes of location, and diversity of experiences amounting to revolutions, the linguistic changes are equally great and rapid. Thus "in the ninth century there existed in Europe no less than seven Romance dialects, all descended from the Latin and all formed after the downfall of the Romain Empire, viz., the Italian, Wallachian, Rhetian, Provençal, Spanish, Portuguese, French." In Italy the change was repeated. For "the population of Rome in the year 1000 spoke a language quite different from that spoken in the time of Constantine, and equally different from that of their descendants."[11]

The general objections to the unity of the race and their descent from a common ancestor, thus disappear before *known* specific facts. And there meets us on the positive side, the following solid array of arguments in support and illustration of the original record, some of them the result only of late researches:

1. Their agreement in all pathological and physiological phenomena, subjects of the same diseases and the same remedies; (2) their similarity of anatomical structure, such that the surgeon educated in New York practises boldly with no changes in Pekin or Australia; (3) similarity in the fundamental powers and traits of mind—so that however degraded any given race may be, intellectually or morally, it has the germs of the highest characteristics and capacity for the highest attainments; (4) similar limits to the duration of life under similar circumstances; (5) the same normal temperature of body and average

---

[11] Southall, "Recent Origin of Man," pp. 28, 29.

rate of pulsation; (6) equal duration of pregnancy; (7) unrestrained fruitfulness between the various races;[12] to which may be added (8) the apparent radiation historically from a common centre in Western Asia; (9) the strong linguistic connections already indicated, binding together races as far removed as from India to Scotland and from Malacca to North America; (10) the common traditions and customs of the races, one of the most remarkable of which is the tradition of the Flood—although by no means the only bond of connection of this kind. As this Biblical announcement of the common descent of the human family long antedated the researches that confirm it, and practically over-rode the proud exclusiveness of many of the nations—the Egyptian lording it over the "vile Khetas" and other tributaries, the Athenian distinguishing himself from the barbarian, and the Chinese from the outside barbarian—so it would appear that every fresh advance of investigation in modern days tends to add to its new confirmation. The arguments for a Pre-Adamite man have not seemed to me important enough to require discussion—in this brief course—and they only make after all an *older Adam.*

[12] The seven points given above are from Delitzsch, "Commentary on Genesis."

On taking leave of the first parents, the sacred narrative traces the line of Cain for some generations before dropping it finally to accompany thenceforth the line of Shem and the "sons of God." A certain similarity in these two lists, either in form or signification, nas led a considerable number of writers to maintain that they were originally the same, and are to be regarded as variations of the same tradition. But here, among other vindicators of the narrative, we find Lenormant, who is free enough in his speculations, coming to the help of Keil and Delitzsch and Kurtz, pointing out the marked differences of real meaning connected with a partial resemblance of form and sound. Thus the Mehujael and the Mahalaleel mean, the one the "smitten of God," the other "praise or splendor of God"; Cain and Cainan "acquisition," and perhaps "smith," Methusael, and Methuselah "man of desire" and "man of the dart"; Irad and Jared "fugitive" and "descent" or "service"; and when the name is the same, as Enoch "initiator," it is capable of a wholly diverse application, the one being the initiator of town life and of the secular arts, the other of religious and spiritual life. While etymologies are more than precarious in these remote ages, we may use Lenormant's suggestion so far forth as to insist on the clear differences which it has been attempted to overlook and confound, and in the two identical instances, Enoch and Lamech, to recognize the well-known law of identical names passing down different branches of the same family as well as in the same family line,—a law so common in the Scriptures and out as to require no special explanation or apology. It may be added that as we know not when the names were given, whether contemporaneously or subsequently, there is a possibility which Delitzsch and Lenormant both suggest, of a naming with reference to the exhibition of a contrast throughout—a partail similarity and real diversity.

When now we attempt to follow down this second line of early consanguinity, the Shemite, with its figures, we find ourselves at once dealing with several extremely difficult and complicated questions, on which in the present state of our knowledge no man can offer an absolute solution, *but only suggestions which look towards a solution*, suggestions to be made with all modesty.

These questions concern the relation of the individuals to each other in the line of succession; the length of life ascribed to them respectively; and the total duration thus indicated from the Creation to the Deluge.

Reversing the order of these questions, there meets us that of the length of time prior to the Deluge, and thereby somewhat directly the duration of man's history on the earth, involved chiefly in this period. For the length of time from the Christian era to the birth of Abraham can be reckoned without any large range of variation—perhaps 200 or 300 years; and the period from Abraham to Noah offers us two Biblical Chronologies (Hebrew and Septuagint) admitting, to some degree, possible confirmatory or corrective collation with semi-historic events. But the previous period stands alone. No figures whatever are offered from any source except the Pentateuch. And the importance of the inquiry shows itself in its bearing on the general question of the antiquity of the human race. I propose to make some modest and cautious suggestions bearing on the inquiry.

To determine the antiquity of the race, then, resort has been had to two sources of inquiry; one, the figures of the Hebrew Scriptures, combined as well as practicable; the other, certain archæological explorations, comparing the relics of man found buried in the surface of the earth with certain other (geological) phenomena and estimating the probable lapse of time required for these phenomena to have taken place. Both these processes are flexible and give us, as will appear, variable results. The Biblical figures are made by intelligent and sober-minded men to vary some hundreds if not thousands of years, according to the method of treatment; while the scientific figures, in the hands of very eminent men, vary not by hundreds or thousands, but by tens of thousands, hundreds of thousands, and, in some estimates, millions of years[18]—a range that is as wild as wide.

It is to be observed, however, that the scientific conjectures for the past few years have been becoming more cautious and much more moderate. Astronomers like Tait and others are ceasing to allow the almost unlimited duration for the present order of things demanded by Darwin and Haeckel. The extreme antiquity of certain attendant and determinative phenomena is become, if not greatly reduced, yet vigorously disputed until such recent writers as Le Conte, while taking a wide range up to a possible 100,000 on one hand come down to 10,000 as the possible limit on the other. And in detail, whereas the actual association of human relics with

---

[13] Le Conte from 10,000 to 100,000, Lubbock 100,000 to 240,000, Draper many hundred thousand years, Prof. Vivien 1,000,000, Dr. Hunt 9,000,000.

those of the mammoth reindeer, cave-bear, cave-lion, cave-hyena, etc., and the supposed great antiquity of the latter, was one strong point, it appears, at least by the concession of Lubbock, Dawkins,[14] and others, that the cave-lion and hyena are not different from living species, but driven *further south*, and the bear, perhaps, not different from the brown bear of Europe; and many circumstances since the discovery of an entire mammoth frozen up in Siberia so perfectly preserved that the wolves, etc., ate up its flesh, and the freshness of a great multitude of other remains, —a reindeer-horn even emitting a fresh odor when cut—have tended greatly to reduce the probable time of the disappearance. Indeed Winchell now remarks,[15] "the contemporaneousness of man with the extinct mammoth is no more proof of man's high antiquity, than the co-existence of the extinct Dodo and the Dutch painter is proof that the Dutchman lived a hundred thousand year ago." The gravel and peat deposites covering the human remains, and the adjacent erosions of the streams, as in the Somme valley, are now shown to have admitted of far more rapid formation than was formerly assigned to them. The

---

[14] Lubbock, p. 289 etc.
[15] "Preadamite Man," p. 436.

vast remoteness of the glacial age—another time-mark in reference to man—has been immensely reduced, with a tendency still in the same direction; Lyell having come down from the date of 800,000 to 200,000 years, Croll from 240,000 to 80,000, while Dr. Andrews of Chicago endeavors to show that the glacial drift of the Northwestern lakes is not older than from 5,300 to 7,500. Southall and Prof. Winchell calculate its disappearance in Wisconsin at a little more than 6000 years ago. Mr. Huxley in 1878 declared the evidence of man prior to the drift to be "of a very dubious character."[16] Meanwhile it has long been seen that to talk of a stone age is to speak of a time perfectly fluctuating, rather than of any fixed or proximate date, inasmuch as the stone age in one race is contemporaneous with the silver and gold of another; thus two hundred and fifty years ago it was all stone age in North America, although 1000 years earlier the mound-builders were using copper; and while all Europe and America have been for these many centuries in the height of the arts, the stone age until very recently had not passed away from the Esquimaux, if it has now. The time is merely relative, and recently Prof. Winchell has ex-

---

[16] Cited in "New Englander," May, 1881.

pressed the belief that in Europe it did not go back further than 2500 or 3000 B. C."[17]

While these variations and amazing reductions have been going on in the interpretation of the one record, questions have been also raised in regard to the other, the Biblical, as to the possibility of its expansion. No questions could legitimately have been raised but for certain striking phenomena attending the numbers themselves. One of these is, as you are well aware, a divergence of the Hebrew, the Greek Septuagint and the Samaritan figures, showing an intentional and systematic set of changes, whereby the Samaritan makes the time from Adam's creation to the flood 1307 years, the Hebrew 1656, the Greek 2262— the difference to the time of Methuselah being made between the last two, by the addition to one or subtraction from the other of 100 years prior to the birth of the son who is named as continuing the line. Continued to the time of Abraham, it makes a difference of about 1400 years. On the whole, the predominant view has been to accept the Hebrew as the true text. But it is to be borne in mind that we have but one Hebrew manuscript as old as the year 580 A. D., and that we in no case seem to get back of a Masoretic revision; while the Septuagint

[17] "Preadamite Man," p. 421.

represents a text which dates 250 years B. C. Whatever the decision as to relative correctness, the phenomenon must raise questions and doubts, as it shows somewhere the hand of the emendator. In addition to this it is noteworthy that we find just ten generations from Adam to Noah as from Noah to Abraham—raising the question whether these may not, as in Matthew's genealogy, have been intentionally equalized by omissions, perhaps in the first series. We cannot make any special account of Lenormant's attempt to convert the whole idea of ten generations into a mythical thing, by comparing traditions of the same number, found by some forcing, among Chaldeans, Assyrians, Iranians, Indians and Egyptians, since these, so far as they have foundation, might be but an echo of the originally known and here recorded fact. But so sound a theological writer as Dr. Frederic Gardiner[18] has endeavored to show from the method of the Pentateuch genealogies themselves that we may possibly understand this record thus; as combining in its extreme brevity two facts in one, viz., "the age in each case of commencing paternity and the name of the particular son by *whom the line* was continued, he not being necessarily the first son, but born at any sub-

[18] "Bibliotheca Sacra," 1873, pp. 323, seq.

sequent time during his father's life." This theory would allow such an addition to the chronology as to make, after deducting 100 years in each case for longevity and infirmity, the extreme possible interval of time from the Creation to the Deluge instead of 1656 to be 6499 years, and the same principle would add some 500 years between Shem and Abraham.[19] In the complications and questions that hang over the whole subject it may be well to bear in mind the possibility of some such solution, should it be necessary. This is quite a different principle of proceeding from the arbitrary decision of Bunsen[20] that these patriarchal lives are merely epochs. Ernst de Bunsen somewhat similarily answers that the name of a person was given to a period[21]—a

[19] "Thus," he says, "Seth might have begun to be a father at 105, but might have actually begotten Enos (by whom the line was continued) at any reasonable time during the 807 years which he afterwards lived; so that the true meaning in the text can be shown by a paraphrase running in this wise; Seth lived 105 years and begat children among whom was Enos; and Seth lived after his beginning to beget children 807 years and begat both sons and daughters, And all the days of Seth were 912 years." I must refer you to his own discussion for the argument.

[20] "Egypt's Place," iv. p. 395.

[21] "Chronology of the Bible," p. 4. He maintains also that "the sum total of the lives assigned to the patriarchs has been shortened by the sum total of the years which

modification of Knobel's view, which finds in Lamech and his sons ethnical personifications or representations of races—and he would add the whole of their lives without even deducting for the time previous to paternity, and reaches a total of 8225 years from Adam to the Flood. These two views are so far forth combined and varied by Rev. T. P. Crawford, that he takes each first statement ("Adam lived 130 years," "Seth lived 105 years") to be the *total* life of each *individual* and supposes the name afterwards in each instance ("All the days of Adam" or Seth) to be used in a family sense—of the special Adamite family till the Sethite family ascendancy.[22] I do not cite these theories to approve them,—although for the theory that a name might represent not a person but a race we certainly find warrant in several of the names in Chapter X., (*e. g.*, Sidon, Canaan, Mizrain, Javan, Madai, etc.) —but to show the possibilities of speculation and explanation upon this abbreviated nar-

each patriarch is recorded to have lived together with his one recorded son," thus reducing an actual period of 8225 years, from Adam to the Flood, to 1656 years. His result it will be observed is greater than that of Prof. Gardiner, reached in a somewhat different way.

[22] Winchell's "Preadamites," p. 450. This gives the same prolongation of time as the theory of Gardiner and De Bunsen.

rative. It is difficult, however, to find any foundation for Lenormant's attempt to convert these lives into *cyclical periods*, on the main hint that Enoch's life was 365 years. Enough perhaps has been said to indicate that we may well be cautious of pledging the Scriptures to an absolute completely and rigid chronology, till we learn further facts.

While making all allowance for possible exigencies, personally I do not as yet see valid reason to adopt any view of the time of man's existence very greatly in excess, if not of Usher's, yet of Hale's Chronology, 5411 B. C. I find that all definite records and distinct traditions go up to a limited distance and stop there, this side even of the date thus gained. Thus the latest and most careful authorities. Chinese investigators now find nothing solid in the antiquity of China earlier than eleven or twelve hundred B. C.; we find no Iranic civilization earlier than 1500 B. C., nor Indian earlier than 1200. The Trojan epoch does not probably reach further than 1200 to 1300 B. C., nor the subjacent cities than 2000. The latest result in regard to Phenicia gives but the sixteenth or seventeenth century B. C. Sayce and Lenormant place the beginning of Assyria about 1500 B. C., and Smith and Lenormant the beginning of Babylon 2300 B. C.

In the case of Egypt one only of the prominent Egyptologists, (Mariette Bey,) insists on finding no contemporaneous dynasties, but makes all successive; and his estimate of 5004 years B. C. to the accession of Menes, still falls within the limits of Hale's Chronology, while Poole's and Wilkinson's estimates subtract more than 2000 years from Mariette's figures.

If it be replied that the Egyptian and Babylonian civilizations first present themselves in a comparatively advanced condition, and therefore suppose a vast preceding interval; we admit the fact, but question the inference, at least in its extent. We *affirm* the striking fact that Egypt comes before us with its pyramids and hieroglyphics, and Babylonia apparently with its four great cities and some degree of skill in the arts. But we maintain that this condition of things in this region best comports with the Biblical record as to the early condition and progress of man, with his attainment in the arts, and the longevity that facilitated that progress by the contemporary accumulation of the fruits of ripened experience. If we accept the Biblical antediluvian narrative as it stands, all eastern history is no longer mysterious, but a simple and natural phenomenon. It is thoroughly consistent with itself and with all known facts. And in this line a very striking coincidence is mentioned, viz.: "Taking as a basis the annual increase of population in France (which has the best statistics for the past two hundred years) at $\frac{1}{217}$ a year, six persons (say Shem, Ham, and Japheth, with their wives) would increase to 1,400,000,000 in 4211 years. But in 1863, the estimated population of the earth was 1,400,000,000, and 4211 years would carry us back from that time to 2348 B. C., the common date of the Flood."[23] And inasmuch as man is always a constructor of permanent memorials, marking in some way the earth's surface, even in his rudest state, in all parts of the world with his structures—dolmens, mounds, stone circles, fortifications or enclosures, excavations, stone huts, and the like, the direct and common sense inquiry is this: if man has been upon the earth all these tens or hundreds of thousands of years, where are those clear marks of that long residence to be found? And echo answers, "Where?"

But on this subject of the early consanguinities as exhibited in the tenth of Genesis, one point I have as yet barely touched,—the extreme longevity of that antediluvian line, which such writers as Bunsen and Lenormant have pronounced intrinsically impossible,[24] and

[23] "New Englander," May, 1881.
[24] Bunsen, "Egypt's Place," iv. 395.

"inconsistent with the physiological conditions of the terrestrial life of man."[25] We do not accept any such arbitrary dictum as deciding the question. Nor do we meanwhile recognize the practicability of escaping the difficulty by supposing a shorter year, such as a month. This would encounter the difficulty of making one patriarch a father at the age of between five and six of our years; and is explicitly precluded by the narrative in the very next chapter, which, while mentioning what took place in the six hundredth and six hundred and first years of Noah's life, gives us also the reckoning of months in the year, up to ten at least, and of days in the month up to twenty-seven. We may content ourselves with the general principle announced by Delitzsch, that "the duration of antediluvian life depended on circumstances and conditions of the earth which our present knowledge cannot reach." Not to suggest that "climate, weather, and other natural conditions may have been quite different" and that "life was much more simple and uniform," we may emphasize the statement that "the after-effects of the condition of man in paradise [destined for immortality] would not be immediately exhausted."

[25] Lenormant, "Contemporary Review," April 1880.

All assertions how long man could live under very different circumstances from those which thousands of years of sin and self-abuse have brought upon him are daring, if not wild. They are as easy to make as they are impossible to prove. There is a respectable English writer who has argued from time to time, I believe in the "Athenæum," that there is no evidence of any life longer than one hundred years. The question is one on which a man dogmatizes, like this man, according to his surroundings and observations.

Ask a man how long a tree will live. If he looks only on a peach-tree, he might say perhaps forty or fifty years; on a grove of poplars or maples, possibly one hundred. Show him the old elm on Boston Common and its history, and he would say three hundred. Let him see the old yew in Fountains Abbey, and he would say five hundred. Let him look on the old olive-trees that stand at the foot of Mount Olivet, and he would add an indefinite number of centuries more. Take him to the fallen Sequoia Gigantea of California, and Mr. Bowles would tell him that the least possible age of one of these is one thousand three hundred and eighty years, and that the mean computation more than doubles that amount. A little additional knowledge would considerably change a man's estimate of what is possible in the life of a tree. Perhaps also of a *man*. Now we must remember how surely all other mechanisms than the living organism are not only impaired, but ruined by misuse; and moreover how even that organism often breaks down, and not only so, but transmits to the generations to come the effects of the misuse, sometimes with accumulations, till certain families are abridged of more than half their life-time as compared with others, and how we inherit the gouts and scrofulas of European ancestry; we have but to consider how better medical and sanitary conditions have within our own knowledge considerably raised the average length of a generation; we have also but to consider what a constant strain is put by most men if not by all men upon the endurance of their vital powers by various irregularities, carelessness, if not positive abuse of their systems, and how these causes have been in operation for ages upon ages in succession,—and I think that instead of wondering that the life, now reduced to a century at the longest, might in the beginning, before all these long and terrible depreciating influences had done their work of ruin, have lasted indefinitely longer, we shall rather say, it could hardly be otherwise. I think that from our knowledge of the human race in its present conditions no man is competent to say how long a life was "intrinsically impossible."

But the most remarkable exhibition of the early affinities is found in the genealogies of the tenth chapter of Genesis. It is a chapter that has furnished the basis of a vast amount of investigation and called forth a singular amount of admiration, being, in Bunsen's language, "the most learned of all ancient documents, and the most ancient among the learned;" or, as Johannes Von Müller puts it, "history has its beginning in this table." It is a theme not for a part of a lecture or a lecture but, as it has been made, for a volume. Nothing like it is to be found in ancient history. And its antiquity is beyond anything but conjecture. In view of all the circumstances we need not be startled at Herder's opinion that the central and original register goes back to about the time of Peleg and the region which he inhabited, in whose time "the earth was divided," when the various races were making their migrations, supplemented, however, in particular lines by the later additions, which come down, as Delitzsch formerly suggested, to the time of Joshua.

Thus, of the progeny of Japheth only two generations are given, but of Shem six. And in this the line of Heber is traced down to the children of Peleg and Joktan, while of Aram only one generation is mentioned. But the very limitations and omissions in many directions are indications of its extreme antiquity. Herder well says, "The very poverty of this chart is its security against being lost or interpolated," and "a pledge of its truth."[26] Thus the Chinese do not appear; for in the time of Moses they had not apparently attained any such prominence as to overcome the obscurity of their distance. And in ascribing Chittim, *i. e.*, Cyprus (and the neighboring coast and islands perhaps) to the line of Javan, or the Ionians, the writer disregards the Phenician colonization as wholly subordinate to the original Greek occupancy of the island as a whole, though the name Chittim is perhaps preserved in the Citium which was one of the chief Phenician cities. Phenicia had not then risen to its commercial influence and power. Indeed the more ancient condition of Phenicia is very distinctly indicated in the absense of all allusion to Tyre, its greatest though later mart, and the mention only of the older Sidon as its representative. Another indication of the same fact is found

[26] Herder, "Spirit of Hebrew Poetry," i. 252, 250.

in the disappearance from all subsequent history of some prominent branches of the lines. Thus among the Shemite race, Eber and Elam and Asshur can be traced distinctly in the Hebrews, Elamites, Assyrians, Syrians; but while Lud is questionable at least, Arphaxad has wholly disappeared. So in other cases. Meanwhile the striking character of the record appears in the circumstance that in all the instances in this branch on which modern science can form a judgment, viz., three of them, it fully coincides with the ancient register in pronouncing them Semitic. So too with the Japhethic races, six in the enumeration, the latest results coincide in affirming, in general, the affiliation here first announced. It finds in Javan, with its subdivisions, the Ionian race; in Gomer, the Cymri and allied tribes of various analogous names, corresponding to the Celtic race; in Madai the Medes; in Magog probably the Scythian tribes; in Tiras broadly the Thracians; in Tubal and Meshech probably the Tibareni and Moschi, that long ago passed away without literature or monuments. But the others are the chief races now thoroughly known to be affiliated,—the common ancestors of the Celts, the Germans, the Sclaves, the Greeks and Romans, the Persians and Hindoos, the great Indo-Germanic, Indo-European, or Aryan family.

Similar in general, though perhaps less distinct and complete are the results reached in regard to the descendants of Ham. But here as throughout the catalogue, the chief difficulty lies in fact that these sources of history lie so far back of all connected secular history, that we lack the means to bridge the chasm.

But any fuller exposition or even comment upon this remarkable record is precluded. My end is subserved in calling special attention to its character, and, above all, to its bond of connection, *the bond of universal consanguinity*. Nothing like it, as I have said, appears in antiquity. On one of the walls at Thebes, is an enumeration of certain nations and tribes, indeed. But they are few, unrelated, and recorded only as the conquests of Rameses the Great. But here, in the words of Dillmann, is "an exhibition of the ultimate relationship of all the nations far and near, outwardly and inwardly so diverse as the weighty thought of this survey. Israel is but one member of universal humanity. All men and nations are of the same race, the same value, and the same consideration, *brethren and kindred*. This Biblical consideration sets out from the greatness and entirety of humanity, before it turns itself to the history of an individual people, the people of God, and then at length by the mouths of the prophets, points forward to the end and ultimate goal of this several history, the union of all nations in the kingdom of God."

That great principle which the illustrious Hungarian exile made his grand text as he traversed this land in 1852—the "Solidarity" of the Nations—was enunciated thousands of years earlier, and in a higher form, in the ancient table of the nations, in the Pentateuch.

LECTURE FIFTH.

THE EARLY MOVEMENTS OF THE NATIONS.

The same record that affirms and traces the original unity of the race, also gives us the oldest and for a long period, yes even now, the only account of its dispersion, its early locations, migrations and movements. We are in a track otherwise untrodden. It is but recently that we have been able fully to test the correctness and value of this ancient source of information. A solitary statement indicates the tendency begun before the Flood, in the wandering of Cain to a region of which we have no further knowledge than the fact. Some writers—even so respectable and conservative an author as Dr. Dawson[1]— have dropped the suggestion that in some of the older stone relics of Europe, and in case of the larger men, like those of Cro-magnon and Mentone, we may have remains of antediluvian times. In some cases the cave-

[1] "Origin of the Earth," p. 299.

dwellers appear to have been destroyed by floods. Other writers (as Bunsen) have called attention to the alleged fact that neither the Chinese nor the Egyptians (almost alone) have any tradition of the Deluge.[2] In Egypt certainly this would not be remarkable, when we consider the nature of the old Egyptian inscriptions,—in no case historical or traditional. They delineate simply current affairs, or are at most tables of royal ancestry. But it is not strictly true either of China or Egypt. China records a *local* deluge at a time differently reckoned as 2062 or 2278 B. C.[3] Egypt exhibits in the tomb of Seti I. the record of a destruction of mankind by the gods in all respects parallel to that of the Pentateuch, except that it was not by a flood —a fact well explained by the Abbé Vigoroux thus, that "inasmuch as an inundation was for them riches and life, they denied the tradition; the race was destroyed in another mode, and the inundation became to them the mark that the anger of Ra was appeased."[4] All speculations on antediluvian races, however, are in the present state of our knowledge superfluous. Nor will I pause to discuss the

---

[2] "Egypt's Place," iii. 379.
[3] Lenormant, "Orig." p. 383.
[4] *Ib.* p. 454.

question how that deluge was brought about; whether, according to the suggestion of Hugh Miller and others, by the gradual subsidence and emergence of a limited area in Asia Minor, say with a radius of 400 miles from a center near Mosul, and thus extending into the Euxine, Caspian and Mediterranean, whereby the inrushing waters would destroy the whole race, not yet dispersed beyond that region; or, with Dawson and others, by the great and general submergence which followed the glacial epoch, and, by general admission, preceded the historical era, and of which traces exist alike in North and South America, in Asia and in Europe.[5] Time may possibly decide the question. Enough if we may, after the flood, look in upon the disintegrations and the crystallizations of the races, in their formative condition and the comparative youth of the world. Nothing could be more interesting than such a study were we able to present it in full. But alas, the race, like the individual, when it arrives at the stage for such investigations, has so far receded from its infantile condition as to have lost the recollection of its infant experience and history.

In the Pentateuch alone are we permitted

[5] Southall, "Recent Origin of Man," pp. 210, 283, 287.

to take such a survey, however limited. Let us turn its unique pages and read what we may in its brief hints.

The earliest post-diluvian indication of national movement is found in the statement (Gen. ix. 19), "These [Shem, Ham and Japheth] are the three sons of Noah, and of them was the whole earth overspread." Next comes the announcement (Gen. x. 2) that one of Eber's sons was named Peleg, "for in his days the earth was divided." Here the simplest interpretation is substantially that of Fürst who says that "here אֶרֶץ stands for יֹשְׁבֵי אֶרֶץ, inhabitants of the earth." A part of the process, as actually begun, is narrated in the next chapter in connection with the tower of Babel, (Chap. xi.). Here we read first of a movement, probably not "*from* the east" but "*eastward*," as it is admissible according both to Gesenius and Ewald to render the phrase, and as Tuch, Delitzsch, Knobel, Wright, Bunsen and others agree (just as in Gen. xiii. 11; iii. 24; xii. 8; ii. 8). It is viewed as eastward from the writer's standpoint in Palestine, to whom the people of Mesopotamia were "sons of the east" (Dillmann), or as it lay, if southerly, also easterly from Armenia (Knobel). The name of the land Shinar, lying eastward, has been within these few years identified (by Lenormant and Sayce) with the Sumir of the Babylonian inscriptions, and is the oldest name, as well as the latest discovered.

From this region we are told God accomplished a still greater movement,—a scattering "abroad upon the face of the earth"—that which was foretokened in the narrative of Noah and described in the "table of the nations." The immediate occasion is given as the confusion of tongues, whereby in a supernatural way was precipitated the change that in due time was sure to come through natural causes. The separation, too, would have been in process of time necessitated. Indeed the movement to the land of Shinar has the appearance of being the first step of that inevitable movement which has been so largely characteristic of early national life: increase of population compelling dispersion, —a swarming of the old hive followed by the pressing and crowding of each last comer upon the heels of its predecessor, till, as in the Aryan movement westward, the Celts were arrested only by the distant shores of the ocean and the islands, and still pressed from behind; or as in this country the older occupants were driven steadily southward.

In this process the distance of the journeyings, the incessant changes and abandonments of all accumulated property, and recedings from the source of supply and from the radiating centers of progress, easily account for the debased conditions of life under which they are often found. Emigration, when incessant, uncorrected and unresisted, tends to barbarism. Those tribes that earliest found and retained their near and permanent abodes, other things being equal, earliest developed and best retained the highest forms of life and art. Such was the case in Chaldea, Babylonia, India, with their fertile and productive plains and mighty streams, and, above all, Egypt with its marvellous position close along the banks of its matchless river of clockwork overflow, and its wonderful facilities and resources, and means of luxury, and also along the eastern and northern parts of the Mediterranean, where everything invited to commerce, to invention and production—climate, soil, minerals and harbors, especially in Phenicia with her two noble harbors in convenient nearness to the trade and civilization of the more ancient East and to the new products of the rising West. The tribes that drove each other through the length of Europe, through its grim forests and over its mountains, across its rushing streams, and through its winter snows, never developed the higher traits of human life till they too at last became stationary, and that was only after they had nearly extinguished what may have been the settled civilization of their earlier home.

Our celebrated table (Genesis x.) shows us something of this process of dispersion, and would show us still more, were we in a condition more fully to interpret it. But unfortunately it is ancient even beyond our reach. Some things, however, stand out very distinct. We have no indication in the Pentateuch indeed what direction the race of Gomer took. Ezekiel, however, brings them "from the north quarter" (xxxviii. 2–6), and we can only find them in the wide-spread names of the Kimmerii, Cymri, and Cambri, in Crimea and Cumberland, etc. But Javan or the Ionians are distinctly relegated to "the isles," or rather maritime regions (which the word includes) "of the Gentiles," and the specifications of the book include the Eolians (Elishah), Tarshish (propably in Cilicia, though some say Spain—Andalusia and Murcia), Cyprus (Chittim) and perhaps the Rhodians, (Dodanim or Rodanim),—to which is added, to indicate their still wider dispersion, "every one after his own tongue, after their families, in their nations" (v. 5). Indeed the vast spread and conspicuous historic influences and activity of the several Japhethic races, of which Javan was foremost, was even more emphatically announced in the utterance of Noah, "God shall enlarge—make wide room for—Japheth, and he shall dwell in the tents of Shem"; as wide room as from India, not only to the western borders of Europe, but to the western borders of America, and now back again to the East, round the globe, and long ago appropriating all the spiritual blessings that dwelt in the tents of Shem. And whether any choose to call this history or prophecy, it is in either case alike distinct.

The direction early taken by the several races is to a considerable extent indicated only by assigning the name of the region to the race. Thus Madai, Sidon, Mizraim respectively designate the Medes and Persians, the Phenicians, and Egyptians. Here Sidon represents the race of which it was the early prominent seat of activity, being mentioned in Joshua as already "great Sidon" (Josh. xi. 8).

And in denominating Sidon "the firstborn of Canaan," the narrative records the great historic fact that at a period estimated (by many) to be some four thousand years ago, "a tribe speaking a Semitic tongue abandoned the nomad habits of their ancestors, and building some rude huts beside a creek, sheltered by an inland breakwater, took to the sea, and called themselves 'Sidonians' or 'Fishermen.' It was a memorable day for humanity, when the first colonizing and commercial power which the world had seen, launched its rude craft tentatively on the Mediterranean. On that day the arts and culture of the East may be said to have set out on their journey to the West, and the long process to have begun by which the sceptre was transferred from the primeval 'river kingdoms' to the republics of the Inland Sea, and from these passed over to the 'ocean empires' of modern times."[6] It was far, far back—it may be five or seven hundred years prior to the greatness of this "Rock" city Tyre (1500 B. C.) which is known neither to the Iliad nor the Odyssey—two hundred years more than that earlier than the occupation of Carthage. Nay, it is supposed that even while Israel was in Egypt[7] the Sidonian mariners, beginning to be crowded by the early Greeks, their pupils and rivals, guided by the pole-star, boldly struck out for the riches of Spain, the tin of Britain and the amber of the Baltic.

How remarkably this narrative antedates all other historic knowledge and fills its gaps, ap-

[6] "Edinburgh Review," Jan. 1882.   [7] *Ib.*

EARLY MOVEMENTS OF NATIONS. 157

pears somewhat conspicuously in regard to Mizraim or the Egyptians, who are here made to radiate from this central stock in Asia through Noah's son Ham. Now "the Egyptians themselves [ancient as they are] appear to have lost the recollection of their origin."[8] Diodorus would refer them to Ethiopia. But the disclosures of the monuments make *Ethiopia* to have been colonized *from Egypt.*[9] The study of the early status and the language brings us to this latest conclusion: "The Egyptian race in its ethnological characteristics is connected with the white population of early Asia: the Egyptian language by its grammatical form with the language called Semitic."[10] Brugsch Bey declares it incontestably proven that the Egyptians originated in Asia. "They must have belonged to the great Caucasian race. With some other nations apparently they form a third branch of it, the Cushite, different in certain peculiarities from the branches called Pelasgic and Semitic.[11] As Maspero expresses himself more fully: "While the Egyptian language, sooner cultivated, was arrested in its development, the Semitic tongues continued thus through long ages, so that if there is evidently a relation of stock between

[8] Maspero, "Histoire Ancienne," p. 13.   [9] *Ib.* p. 14.
[10] *Ib.* p. 16.   [11] "Histoire d'Egypte," pp. 5, 6.

the language of Egypt and those of Asia, the relation is distant enough to leave to this people a distant physiognomy.[12] He calls it "proto-Semitic." This would bring them into the relation indicated in the Pentateuch, early emigrants from Asia and connected in language with at least the Canaanites, according to the received views, including the Phenicians. I will not follow Maspero (after De Rougé) in the designation of the several descendants or tribes of Mizraim to their respective localities from the hieroglyphic records—as when he makes the Ludim to be the Routou or Loudou, or Egyptians proper, Anamim the Anou or inhabitants of On of the north (Heliopolis) and On of the south (Hermonthis), Lehabim the Lybians, Natuphim No-Phtah on the north of Memphis, the Pathrusim, the Pa-to-res, midlanders between Memphis and the first cataract.[13] These may be considered as too precarious, however striking.

Again the Canaanite tribes in other portions of the Pentateuch are located in detail, and they are found scattered over the whole region from Sidon to Gaza, and on the east to the Ghor at an unknown point, Lasha. Here we find our only distinct knowledge of a family of tribes—including the warlike Kheta or

[12] "Histoire Ancienne," p. 17. [13] *Ib.* p. 14.

Hittites of the Egyptian monuments—once numerous and powerful, who fought well for their strongholds, till they were overpowered by a mightier destiny, and disappeared without a vestige, unless it be found in the troglodyte caves of the south, in certain names not yet displaced, and perhaps in the language they may have imparted to the long tolerated and afterward dominant Hebrew race, and in certain few inscriptions about the Orentes, not yet deciphered.

One of the most noteworthy statements of this earliest record is that in regard to Nimrod—so remote indeed that though identified by George Smith with the Izdhubar of the Babylonian tablets, the latter is by others (Sayce and Lenormant) remanded to the sphere of legends. He was a Cushite and "the beginning of his kingdom was Babel and Erech and Accad and Calneh in the land of Shinar. And out of that land he went forth and builded Nineveh and the city of Rehoboth and Calah and Resen between Nineveh and Calah, the same is a great city." It is not my purpose to disentangle the construction and details of this brief and difficult statement, but to notice the career of early conquest and construction thus briefly indicated. This rearing of certain great cities in

Shinar by a Hamitic, Cushite monarch who also pushed his way into Asshur, which region however was *assigned to the family of Shem*, and from which Abram actually originated—presents not only a record of early national enterprise, but a mingling of national elements, not disentangled till in very recent times, and now perhaps but in part. But thus much appears to be settled. The name Shinar is the same with the Sumir of the inscriptions, now revived in the name applied to the Sumirian language and race, which is also by some identified with, and by others distinguished from, the Accadian, and belongs to a Scythian or Turanian race, which seems by modern researches to have preceded the Assyrian and Chaldean races in these regions. They were the original proprietors of the cuneiform alphabet. The latest researches also show, by their side or as their successors on this soil, a powerful Cushite race as set forth in the sacred narrative.[14] But at an early date it is also certain that a Semitic race, represented by the inscriptions in the Assyrian language, was found on the soil of Chaldea, whom some (Geo. Smith) have supposed to have mastered the earlier Turanians even before this

---

[14] Maspero, "Histoire," p. 145.

Cushite invasion. It is difficult to determine relative dates. But the fundamental fact of the record has emerged in recent times, that the three great families, Shem, Ham and Japheth, were early and strangely mingled on this ancient territory. It was hinted at long after by the Chaldean historian Berosus: "There were at first a great number of men of different races who had colonized to Chaldea."[15] And this early mingling of races in Chaldea in part accounts for the difficulties that overhang the question of the so-called "Semitic" tongues, which evidently were spoken by some non-Semitic nations. The complication would seem to have been increased or continued by subsequent proximities or interminglings of the Semitic and Hamitic races, as in Palestine, Northern Africa, and perhaps in Arabia and Abyssinia[16] —the record in the first two cases being also furnished in the Pentateuch. In the city Accad remains a relic of the name by which one portion of the early Turanian people and their speech were known—Accadian; and as some aver in its significance "mountain" (as contrasted with Sumir, "plain") a reminiscence of the mountainous region of Ar-

---

[15] Tompkins, "Times of Abraham," p. 7.
[16] *Ib.* p. 52.

menia which was their still earlier home.[1] Let me only add that of the ancient Erech we have the well-known primitive ruins in the mounds of Warka.

It was from this land of Chaldea, south of Babylonia, and from its ancient city of Ur, now identified beyond reasonable doubt with Mugheir, that the most eventful migration took place that the world has seen—that of Abram, the Hebrew. With him came up the spiritual hopes and destinies of the nations. It is not impossible that the aggressions of Elam, of which the same record gives the oldest information, may have enforced the divine call "to get him forth." He followed up the Euphrates by the route so common in ancient times, the earliest known traveller over that famous route, in preference to a journey across the difficult western desert, and for some unknown reason he paused in Charran. The time appears from many indications to have been one of very general unrest among the nations. And while he was in Charran, it has been shown that the host of "Chedorlaomer and his tributaries must have marched through to their distant conquests," and "Abram's eyes probably looked upon the long array of Elam, Larsa, Shinar and Goiim,

---

[17] Lenormant, "Chaldean Magic," p. 360.

with which thirteen years later he was so suddenly to be engaged in deadly conflict."[18] We follow him next down through the land of Syria over the great route, now first mentioned in history, by Damascus, (also first appearing here and represented in his steward, Eliezer of Damascus), passing "through the land," the oldest Palestinian traveller on record, pausing at Shechem at the plain or rather the oaks of a place now emerging into history, and again at a point between Bethel and Ai, and so onward south. When the famine finds him, he pushes on over that immemorial route, now first indicated, through the south country to Egypt, and gives us the first historic glimpse of the civilization of that mighty people. We find him, and afterward his son, in the Negeb, or South country, of which we know through them and through those remarkable ruins and relics alone, that it was once filled with cultivation and population. It had already received its geographic name Negeb, which appears a little later as "Nekeb" among the conquests of Thothmes III. With him once more we stand at Bethel, and with Lot we look from the sightly eminence east of Bethel over the land of Palestine, and see the fertility of the tropical plain below, in its wicked civilization. With Abram's eye

[18] Tompkins, p. 58.

of faith we also look from the place where he was, "northward and southward and eastward and westward," over the land of distant promise. The whole scene stands out before us, by glimpses, in connection with this personal history of those times; later described in the same Pentateuch as "a good land, a land of brooks of water, of fountains and depths that spring out of the valleys and hills, a land of wheat and barley and vines and fig-trees and pomegranates, a land of oil olive and honey" (Deut. viii. 7); now in Abraham's time a pastoral country in great measure, sprinkled with flocks and herds, and traversed already by a great travelled route from north to south, tending to Egypt, apparently with its stages and halting places even then somewhat as now. The whole scene is before our eyes. Here and there as at Hebron, Shechem, Jerusalem, some tribe had made its central seat, probably as yet with little show of fortification. Of one of these, Hebron, curiously enough, we have the very date given, "seven years older than Zoan of Egypt." The main portion of the territory would seem to have been otherwise then open for the unhindered passage of a military force. But the chief permanent population was apparently outside the mountainous centre of Palestine—along the coast around Sidon, in the Ghor where were Hazezon Tamar and the cities of the plain —Sodom being even a city with "a gate"— beyond the Jordan from Ashteroth Karnaim to Mt. Seir and El Paran, as well as about Damascus north, and around Beersheba, in Gerar and the region south of Palestine. They could, as at Kirjath Arba, convey land by regular sale "with the trees thereon." Here and there the eye falls on oak or terevinth groves, as at Shechem, Mamre and El Paran. Beersheba may have been as destitute of trees then as to-day; for there Abram planted a grove or a tree,—an act which as clearly distinguishes him from the Arab Sheikh of Dean Stanley, as did the wells which he and Abimelech dug at Beersheba. In this bird's-eye glimpse of the location of the nations in Palestine, there comes before us one remarkable character,—a veritable priest of the Most High God,—one who, outside the line of Abram had so kept alive the sacred fire that Abram himself was blessed by him and paid him tithes. It is a strangely suggestive apparition; without recorded father or mother, beginning of priestly years or end of days, he passes before us like a bird darting through a lighted room, from the dark into the dark again

In Abram's favorable reception in Egypt we perhaps get a glimpse of the Asiatic relation already begun in the conquest by the Hyksos or Shepherd Kings of Egypt. For Brugsch Bey now derives these Hyksos from Elam and Media, averring that he has found the Egyptain name of "Menti" applied to those localities. The national departure had taken place already. And if we suppose that the oppressive influences in their own neighboring home had sent forth these singular adventurers to Egypt, we can understand the sympathetic bond which secured the patriarch an honorable welcome in Egypt and a safe departure, though rightly rebuked. The same tendency to Egypt and kindly reception which is here narrated is also illustrated in that famous picture of the Asiatic company of thirty-seven Amu honorably received in the days of Osirtasen II., and whom Lepsius has perhaps rightly described as the "predecessors of the Hyksos," a "mighty Hyksos family who pray to be received into the blessed land, and whose descendants perhaps opened the gates of Egypt to the Semitic conquerors allied to them by race."[18] This could not have been relatively many years—possibly two centuries—before Abram's own reception.

[19] Lepsius, "Letters from Egypt," p. 112.

Meantime from the Egyptian side of this migratory and predatory movement, Abram's history once more carries us to the eastern side, from whence the tribes were thus already crowding on their neighbors. Some years later—we know not how many—we find the king of Elam and his confederates enforcing a previous tribute upon the distant tribes of Palestine. We will not pause to inquire whether the name Chedorlaomer, can be identified with Kudur-Mabuk, or Kudur-Lagamar, as Mr. Tompkins still supposes. But of these nations thus allied we find the king of Elam now at the head, as the liege lord and master; for it was he whom the five cities of Palestine had served for twelve years and against whom they had now rebelled. Accordingly we find it recorded in the annals of Assurbanipal, king of Assyria, that only in his day had he, the king of Assyria, by conquest of Elam brought back from Susa an image of Nana which an Elamite monarch (Kudur-nankhundi) had carried off from Babylonia 1635 years before, *i. e.*, near three hundred years prior to Abram's emigration. It had been a long-established ascendancy and aggressiveness *of Elam* and at length in Abram's time it had swept across the desert into Syria and Palestine. With this powerful Elamite king was now associated, as his inferior and ally only, the king of Shinar. Arioch king of Ellasar was also of the company. And, curiously enough, not only has *his* capital city Larsa (now Senkereh on the east of the Euphrates) been identified, but Eriaku, the same with the Hebrew Arioch, is found to be the son of Kudur-Mabuk and to have dwelt in Larsa. The fourth of these royal aggressors, Tidal king of "Goiim," is less definitely localized either in the narrative or the inscriptions, Guti or Gutium, both of which sources favor the idea that his monarchy was over less consolidated tribes to the north. But in striking correspondence to and explanation of this consecutive narrative, the inscriptions disclose great expeditions of Kudur-Mabuk and Arioch, with conquests in Syria, whereby the former attained the title "lord of Martu" *i. e.*, of the god of the West; and Rawlinson, Sayce and Lenormant all bring the date singularly close to the time of Abraham (Rawlinson 2100 B. C., Sayce 2000, Lenormant "approximately to the time of Abraham."[19] This tale of conquest might apply to the time twelve years before when the valley kings were made tributary, probably in the greater campaign through Syria as well as Palestine. For in the second campaign a more humiliating fate awaited them.

[20] Tompkins, "Times of Abraham," p. 180.

We follow these fighting nations this second time as they come, evidently in force, over the commercial and military track, ascending the valley of the Euphrates and crossing it at Bir, or more likely at Jerabolus, the ancient Carchemish, pushing south-westerly over the deep valley of the Orontes at "the entrance of Hamath" (twice mentioned in our Pentateuch)—that ancient place where are found strange inscriptions perhaps of the veritable Hittite race. Passing by Damascus, out of our sight, they emerge on the east side of Jordan in Bashan, striking first the Rephaim at an unknown point, then the Zuzim,—wholly lost to history—at Ham, probably Hamitat, just east of the Dead Sea, then Shaveh Kiriathaim, "the plain of the two cities," now also lost out of knowledge unless the name of the tribe of Emims be found in the travels of Mohar, "Mat-amim," land of Emim. Then we find them at Seir among the Horites, the troglodytes. They had taken what is since, and may have been then, the great commercial route to Arabia. Still they pushed on down along the route of the Ghor to El Paran, not now definitely known, but "by the wilderness." What was their aim here? The old Egyptian mines, long wrought already? We can only guess. But they returned by Kadesh—whether the Ain Kades of Williams, the Ain el Weibeh of Robinson, or some still unknown place. It was a long expedition, and must have called for no little skill in the arrangement, as well as vigor in the prosecution. And now having cut off all the surrounding sources of help, they struck what we may suppose were the *rich* cities of the plain—for here, at a later date, in Jericho it was that Achan hid his prize, the wedge of gold and the goodly Babylonish garment or mantle. They carried off the spoil. And here the very geography and condition of the region is put on record. It was a valley, and bitumen pits were there—where bitumen still is found—and a mountain region for the survivors to escape.

When Abram joined himself to Aner and Eshcol to retake his nephew Lot, by a sort of poetic justice he was arming himself against the aggressors that had oppressed his own native land of Chaldea. And in his military tactics, he showed himself worthy to have been reared—as he was—in the midst of warlike times. From the opposite range of hills, no doubt—the bold headlands of Naphtali, south of lake Huleh,—he could, as he approached, see the enemy resting in security and carousing over his spoil. By an almost

Napoleonic promptness and skill he advanced upon them in detachments, struck them by night, and routed them beyond Damascus.

With this thorough discomfiture of the former chief oriental monarch of the time, of which, of course, no record ever will be found in the boastful inscriptions of Babylonia or Assyria, the *public* movements in and around the old hive of the nations are left in silence for many centuries. For although later in the life of Abraham, and again through twenty years of the life of Jacob, we are permitted to look into the heart of Padan Aram, it is exclusively a vision of rural and family scenes, without a reference to the monarchy or the government, except as Laban asserts in one instance a controlling custom of the country.

Not so meanwhile in other lands. We have here the only narrative concerning the origin of that race that have left their sole mementoes in the forsaken ruins of Moab. Here also the early days of that powerful race that once warred upon Judea, pillaged her capital, by the hand of its Edomite monarch, Herod, struck at the life of the infant Jesus, and left its weird city Petra to be discovered in our own day in the cleft of the rocks, in ghastly desolation.

Here also alone are exhibited the great

Arab race in their origin, their characteristics, their early central location, and their long and peculiar history. The sons of Ishmael had their dwelling "from Havilah unto Shur that is before Egypt *as thou goest* toward Assyria,"—where we observe the distinct implication of early travel and communication between the two lands,—in the region where the traveller now looks upon the sons of Ishmael in their purest, almost primitive type. The roving Bedouin to-day fulfils that marvellously descriptive prophetic utterance, "He shall be a wild-ass man; his hand shall be against every man and every man's hand against him; and he shall dwell in the presence of his brethren." And from Havilah to Shur you behold him to-day, as roving and untamed as the wild ass, and dwelling in the presence of his brethren. "Until to-day the Ishmaelites are in undisturbed, free possession of the great peninsula lying between the Euphrates, the Isthmus of Suez and the Red Sea, from whence they have spread over wide districts in Northern Africa and Southern Asia" (Delitzsch). Ishmael has also become, according to this prophetic utterance, a great nation, and more than "twelve princes" have sprung from his stock. "Every addition to our knowledge, of Arabia and its inhabitants," says Kalisch, "confirms more strongly the Biblical statements. While they have carried their arms beyond their native lands, and ascended more than one hundred thrones, they were never subjected to the Persian empire. The Assyrian and Babylonian kings had a transitory power over small portions of their tribes. Here the ambition of Alexander the Great and his successors received an insuperable check, and a Roman expedition in the time of Augustus totally failed. The Bedouins have remained essentially unaltered since the times of the Hebrews and the Greeks." Is it not one hundred and twenty millions that speak the Arabic tongue to-day?

Passing at a bound over some two hundred years from Abraham's time, the Pentateuch opens up another panorama of historic vision. I will not pause to dwell upon the unfolding of the one central people, and the sharp defining of the whole career and institutions that have so ineffaceably stamped their intense nationality to the present day. Few men consider what an irreparable loss to the world's records would be the obliteration of that long and eventful history from the world's on-goings, or with what singular and absolutely unparalleled definiteness it is given us, from its incipient stages. And not only as a clear record of a wonderful national growth and source of moral illumination to the world is it a κτῆμα ἐς ἀεί, but meanwhile how its pages beam with life, and what strange personages walk across its scenes in all their distinctness of delineation: the mighty and majestic Father of the faithful, the wary and versatile head of the twelve tribes, ripening at last to venerableness and beauty, the fleckless Joseph and the colossal law-giver, —how they stand out like sunbeams on our sight.

And as we follow their journeyings we are still enveloped with the movements of the nations. We fall upon the line of early international trade at Dothan, where the Midianite or Ishmaelitish merchants are moving towards luxurious Egypt with their camels, bearing spices and balm and myrrh, perhaps for the kitchen, the toilet, the medicine chest, and the tomb, and where they pause by the way to buy cheap a slave for the house of "the Captain of the guard." In Egypt we may not pause to look around upon the vivid scenes of sumptuous court life here delineated, ages before they emerged upon modern sight from the tombs. But we get clear hints of the great national movements of which we are in search,—hints quite as significant as would be more detailed statements. The elevation of a foreigner such as Joseph to a high office, suggests the fact of Egypt being then in the hands of foreign invaders, the Hyksos; while the solicitude to provide the Israelites a home in Goshen, remote from the old native Egyptian population, and because "every shepherd is an abomination to the Egyptians," suggests the smouldering and growing hatred of that dynasty, that only waited for its time under Ahmes to drive them forever from the land. The reiterated intimation to the ten brethren, "Nay, ye are spies; to see the nakedness of the land ye are come," hints at a growing sense of insecurity and governmental suspicion, strongly aroused and fully justified.

When at length, long after Joseph's death, another king or dynasty arose which knew not Joseph, we are reminded at once of that native dynasty of Memphis to whom the eventful story of Joseph with his relations at On was unknown and certainly uncared for. And when after the lapse of centuries, the children of Israel are ground down with their labors on the strongholds of Egypt, we are reminded of that line of fortresses which Seti I. and Rameses II. found it needful to string along the eastern border of Egypt. For the intermediate conquests of the great warrior, Thotmes III. had long passed by, and Rameses, with all his boasting of victories, had roused enemies whom he feared. And when the sceptre passed or was to pass into the hands of the feeble Meneptha, we can well understand those recorded apprehensions "lest they [the Israelites] multiply, and it come to pass that when there falleth out any war they join also unto our enemies and fight against us." We see also the explanation of that great body of troops with which, in its military but weakened condition, the monarch found it needful to stand always provided, and which at a day's warning was in readiness to follow on the track of Israel. The horsemen and chariots speak of a great national change since the days of camels and asses—since the time of Abraham. Possibly also in the children of Israel's march out of Egypt in orderly array, חֲלֻשִׁים, and in the division on the march into thousands and hundreds with their captains (Num. xiv. 31)—into regiments and companies with their regular commanders,—we are to recognize an echo of the military discipline that now filled the once peaceful kingdom, as it does Germany to-day, and that responded to the warlike movements now thoroughly aroused and setting toward the ultimately doomed country which was to be the spoil of the nations.

And on the march of Israel we encounter a changed state of affairs from the day when not only did the ten brothers pass quietly over the old caravan road, that even a solitary woman had once attempted alone with her child, Ishmael. For this great host were deliberately turned toward the Red Sea instead of the shorter way "through the land of the Philistines" to Canaan, "lest peradventure the people repent when they see war, and they return to Egypt" (Ex. xiii. 17). The change was great indeed. The powerful Amalekites encounter them desperately on the way, although the Egyptian forces at the mines seem not to have molested them, and victory was gained for Israel only after a hard-fought battle. Edom also bristled with warlike preparations and defiance. When the misguided nation would have pushed their way north from Kadesh, they were driven back in great discomfiture by the Amalekites; and who can tell but that the oldest portion of the ruined fortresses on the top of Meshrifeh may be part of the stronghold of Zephath, or Sebaita "on the hill top," from which these "Canaanites smote them even unto Hormah." When at length the weary journey had brought the nation by a circuitous route upon the flank of the promised land, even here were new and strange preparations. Jericho was now enclosed with its walls. The hills of Palestine were covered with strongholds, and filled with fighting men. And it was only after a long and bitter struggle of conquest that the warrior Joshua rested on his arms, and the blessings from Gerizim and the curses from Ebal came swelling and thundering over the heads of the people as they stood awe-stricken in the vale of Shechem below; and the nation had peace, although many of its surrounding foes still remained to be thorns in its side.

Thus striking in themselves, significant in their relations, and eventful in their issues, are the national movements recorded in this ancient history. We catch, not a glimpse, but a clear and steady look into scenes and events so far away as to be completely lost out of sight. We gaze on the dead past and it comes to life. It is as though through the vacant space we point some great telescope toward a seeming blank and there rises before us a new unseen planet, not offering us a dreary range of extinct volcanoes and waterless plains, but filled with verdure and activity, with living men and women engaged in all their daily round. Scenes of terror, of pathos and of joy; the march of armies, the clash of arms, the shout of the victor, and the cry of the vanquished; the voice of the bridegroom and the lament of the widowed and the defiance of the criminal; the stern command of the mighty despot and the beating of the poor downtrodden slave; the firm tread of the individual hero, the quiet footfall of the moving caravans, the tramp of the nations as they march to their early and perhaps their later homes, the din and bustle of a young world hurrying hither and thither with struggle and confusion and strife, come reverberating down the distant centuries as clear and fresh, and yet as softened too, as the mingled sounds from some village below rise through the evening air to the ear of the wanderer, as he pauses to listen on the neighboring height.

LECTURE SIXTH.

THE EARLY DOCUMENTS.

It would seem to be hundreds of years, and yet it is less than forty, since even so good a scholar as Prof. Norton[1] of Harvard College could publish to the world his doubts, after Gesenius and De Wette, whether the art of alphabetical writing was known, or so far advanced in the time of Moses as to admit of his being the author of the Pentateuch. On the contrary, the date of the discovery recedes beyond all knowledge, and disappears in the mist. In Egypt the cautious Wilkinson finds the hieroglyphic writing upwards of 2500 years B. C., and passing into the hieratic about 2240 B. C.; Lepsius, with larger numbers, speaks of a "perfectly formed system and a universal habit of writing between three and four thousand years before Christ." In Chaldea the cuneiform inscriptions ascend to at least the

[1] Norton's "Genuineness of the Gospels," vol. ii. Note D., p. c. Second Ed., 1848.

time of King Lig-bagas, assigned by some (H. C. Tomkins) to 2700, and by Sayce[2] to about 3000 years before the Christian era. It is mostly syllabic, and is considered to have been derived from hieroglyphic signs of its own.

It is from the Egyptian hieroglyphics, directly or through its hieratic form, as is now generally conceded, that the Phenician and thence the Grecian alphabet came—the alphabet, properly so-called, of *letters*, fixed. "M. de Rougé," says Maspero, "proved that at the time when the Shepherds reigned in Egypt, the Canaanites had selected, among the forms of cursive writing, a certain number of characters corresponding to the fundamental sounds of their language. His demonstration, reproduced in Germany by Lauth, Brugsch and Ebers, was considered decisive, and the results have been generally accepted. The Phenician alphabet is composed of twenty-two letters, of which fifteen are so little changed that we recognize at a glance their Egyptian prototype, and the remainder ascend to the hieratic type without violence to the laws of probability."[3] This adaptation was the work of a business people, and a stroke of commer-

[2] "Chaldean Genesis," p. 24.
[3] Maspero, "Histoire Ancienne," p. 600.

cial genius. "The Phenician alphabet," continues Maspero, "first used in Canaan, became modified according to localities, and formed successively the Aramean, Palmyrene, and Hebrew alphabets. Carried by the Sidonians and Tyrians into the countries where commerce led them, it became the common stock from which were detached all [nearly all] the alphabets of the known world from India and Mongolia to Gaul and Spain"—not including the extreme east and extreme west.

How early the Phenician or Canaanite—which is of course the Hebrew—alphabet was in use, we cannot tell. It was in use in Canaan, say the Egyptologists, during the Hyksos dynasty. Nor can we say with absolute confidence how early any of the matters contained in the earlier part of the Pentateuch were committed to writing. There is not only ingenuity but weight in the suggestion of Herder[4] that such lists of names as form the early genealogical tables carry with them the necessity of writing to preserve them. He even suggests, and not without show of reason, that the very effort to preserve such tables may have been the necessity which led to the invention of early writing. "If," says he, "alphabetic writing

[4] Herder's "Spirit of Hebrew Poetry," i. 254–7.

was ever to be invented, it must be brought about by reason of something simple, something very definite and very indispensable, which could not be expressed by images. Now names exhibit these very conditions; and it is a fact that names and genealogical registers constitute the earliest traditions of the primeval world." He suggests that the fifth chapter of Genesis may have been, with its names and numbers, the first tablet of thought in articulate sounds and "transmitted through Noah to Shem, as the meaning of the latter name might denote." If we do not fully adopt this opinion, we may recognize the seemingly insuperable necessity that such a series of otherwise disconnected words should be handed down by written record. "These registers," Herder strikingly remarks, "are the historical archives of the Orientals, and the historical traditions are the commentary." And in speaking of the history before the Deluge he says, "it passes obviously into a mere record of significant names, genealogical records and family traditions mingled together; and here too its poverty is a pledge of its truth."[5]

If the Phenician alphabet was introduced into Palestine only in the time of the Shepherd

[5] *Ib.* i. p. 254.

Kings of Egypt, it would appear that though Abraham would have found it already there, yet he did not learn it there; for he himself came up from a land that had known the art of writing some hundred years—five hundred, if we were to adopt Sayce's date—earlier than the earliest of those Kings [about 2200 B. C., the beginning of the Shepherd reigns, according to Brugsch]. How far back in the line of Abraham's ancestry written memorials of the kind indicated may have existed, we can hardly even conjecture. There is nothing incredible in the supposition that writing may have been an antediluvian invention, but some things to favor it. Surely the general skill in the arts would be in keeping with it; the very process of constructing a vessel five hundred and seventeen feet long would imply some species of notation; and the genealogical tables, with the definite numbers, in the fifth of Genesis, would seem almost to have necessitated it. And a noticeable indication of evident but fossilized mistake in copying, (which however would naturally have been limited to a script like the Hebrew or Phenician,) is found in Gen. iv. 18, where מְחוּיָאֵל is changed at once to מְחִיָּאֵל.

And let me here remark in passing that the admission of such ancient genealogies into the Pentateuch is no more peculiar than the admission of the much longer genealogies, evidently from the tribal records, into the Gospels of Matthew and Luke. Indeed the similarity of the phenomena might indicate similarity of origin and give color to the suggestion of Herder that in the genealogies of Genesis v. we have the transcript of an early recorded table.

It is not difficult to fix at once upon other portions of the early history which have the appearance of coming down from a far greater antiquity than the time of Moses, substantially in their present form. Without seeking for other possible instances in the preceding narratives with their ἅπαξ λεγομενα, the mind fixes at once on the account of the Deluge, and that of Abraham's warlike expedition. In the history of the Deluge, when one reads not merely the steady announcement of definite numbers, and that not alone in the dimensions of the ark, the time of the rain and of the prevalence of the water, and the height of the water, the several intervals of waiting and the age of Noah, but the reiterated, minute and emphatic exactness, such as the six hundredth year, second month, seventeenth day of the month " in the bone of that day," the seventh month and seventeenth day of the month, tenth month and first day, six hundred and first year, first month, first day, second month, seven and twentieth day—and still more all the marks of a personal beholding and participation, as when the waters increased and first "bare up the ark" and "it was lifted up above the earth," then the waters prevailed and increased "greatly, greatly" till "the ark walked upon the face of the waters," and still they prevailed "till all the high hills under the whole heaven were covered," and the mountains were covered—then how the waters decreased, and in the first day of the month "the tops of the mountains *were seen;*" then all the vivid minuteness of detail, *opening the window* to send the raven, and afterwards the dove, putting forth his hand and pulling her in unto him, sending her once more and on her return "*lo*, in her mouth an olive-leaf fresh-plucked"—once more removing the covering, looking, "and *behold* the face of the ground was dry"—I say, in all the exactness and minuteness of this pre-Raphaelite painting, how can one fail to feel the presence of a contemporary record, or, as some have called it, a log-book. And furthermore, when one considers the exactness of statement in regard to such a multiplicity of details, and contrasts the sobriety and consistency of this simple narrative, with the dimness, the inconsistencies and the extravagances of that multitude of traditional accounts of the Deluge that are found scattered through every part of the world, it is not easy to see how it could have been thus kept in its integrity except as placed on record at no distant date from the transactions so carefully recorded.

So of the fourteenth chapter of Genesis —when one looks at its wholly *detached* completeness, at its several peculiarities of diction and utterance, including its mention of Abraham as "the Hebrew," and especially at the double set of names whereby terms which were obsolete in Moses' time are explained by their later equivalents, coming down, however, no further than his day, unless in the case of Dan,—not difficult of explanation,—he cannot well dissent from Ewald's statement that "all the indications tend to show that this whole piece was written prior to the time of Moses."[6] These are specimens of what may be freely admitted in many other instances less noticeable, to whatever extent clear indications may demand. Although there is now a strong tendency to accept the theory of certain leading minds, and recog-

---

[6] "Geschichte von Israel," vol. i. p. 80, Note.

nize an Elohist, two Jehovists, a Deuteronomist, and one, *or more*, "redactors," yet certainly nothing can be more dreary and bewildering than the attempt to harmonize or even to tabulate the diversities in the assignment of the respective contributions, from the time of Astruc to that of Dillmann.

And here let it be observed that the acceptance and incorporation of such earlier true narratives into the history, no more militates against the proper Mosaic authorship of that history, than the introduction of large extracts from Bradford or Morton, or other and later sources of contemporary information, interferes with the proper authorship of a history of the United States by Bancroft; and when this latter historian, recording with quotations a condensed statement of the establishment of Fort du Quesne (iv. 117) adds "where now is Pittsburgh," he almost exactly imitates the Hebrew historian, in Gen xiv. with a mere substitution of the English idiom.[7]

[7] Thus Professor C. A. Briggs, who somewhat distinctly assents to the general analysis of the Pentateuch and Joshua into four principal documents combined by a "redactor" or editor and compiler, makes this very decided statement: "There is nothing in this variation of documents as such to require that they should be successive and separated by wide intervals, or that would prevent their being nearly contemporaneous. There is nothing

THE EARLY DOCUMENTS. 189

It may also be added that very probably the incorporation of earlier narratives explains many characteristic forms of phraseology, and will, as has been so often argued, *in part* account for the diverse names of God which appear conspicuously in the earlier part of the Pentateuch. I say, in part. For so far as appears, no theory that has been advanced fully explains the facts. For after more than three quarters of a century of the ablest and most searching discussion, the following facts are to be observed: (1) The lack of any absolute or general agreement among the anatomists of the Pentateuch as to the number of parts of which it is formed; (2) still less agreement in the assignment of the several portions to their supposed originals; (3) and no thoroughly self-consistent theory of a supposed methodical combination of documents in whatever mode, has yet been

in this distinction of documents as such that forces us to abandon the Mosaic age as the time of their origin. The fault of the supplementary and the crystallization hypotheses, is in their attempts to determine the *order* and fix the time of the genesis of those various documents that constitute our Pentateuch and spread them over the various periods of the history of Israel. The evidences on which these theories are built, are exceedingly precarious." "Pres. Rev." vol. iv. p. 100. To these faults he might also add, with equal force, the attempt to determine precisely the limits of the documents employed.

broached—unless it is some such "supplementary hypothesis" as virtually recognizes one proper author. Without attempting here the details of a volume or volumes, it is sufficient to say that all these theories, however dexterously adjusted, break down in the application in some or all of the following modes: (*a*) the actual presence and sometimes preponderance in one alleged document of terms pronounced characteristic of a different one, as where the name of Jehovah prevails over that of Elohim in an Elohistic passage, especially in the later books of the Pentateuch; (*b*) the abrupt introduction of alleged characteristic words in narratives alleged to be of a different origin (as Jehovah, Gen. vii. 16, xvii. 1, and many other words and phrases); (*c*) the continual abundant cross references of each respective portion to statements contained in the other alleged class of documents —as of the Elohistic to the Jehovistic, and *vice versa;* (*d*) and finally, excessive and unreasonable dissections and dismemberments of closely connected passages, required in order to make even this show of a case.[8]

[8] Thus, Gen. xxxvii. has thirty verses which Davidson (after Boehmer) divides into thirty-two fragments, and Knobel into nine. Gen. xli. is analyzed by Davidson into forty-two fragments, by Knobel into twenty-two, and

And a man of sober judgment, while freely admitting the use of other materials, yet when he ponders the diverse and ever-changing hypotheses, the conflicting results, and especially the arbitrary devices by which they are largely maintained, as well as the uses to which they are applied, may be pardoned for questioning whether the great body of these bold speculators are not more earnestly bent on establishing an ingenious theory than ascertaining the very truth. For be it observed, we do not dispute the use of previous material, by whatever of several names designated, though we may demur to the unwarranted inferences from it, and the capricious minuteness of the schemes that are erected upon it.

Nor, on the other hand, can we insist on the opinion that the characteristic names of God, for example, were in each and every case selected in accordance with some conscious plan. Doubtless in many instances a

by Dillmann (Knobel's editor in 1875) it is regarded as chiefly by one writer with nine insertions, sometimes of a verse and twice of two or three words only. Schrader (in 1876) finds in ch. xlvii. some nine different portions, although in two instances (vs. 11 and 27) they consist each of *two words* from the Elohist, etc. Meanwhile and last of all Kuenen and Wellhausen come forward to reverse all preceding dates and make the Elohistic portions later than the Jehovistic.

definite reason existed for using (for example) the name of Jehovah as the God of revelation and of covenant. Thus we may, if we choose, suppose, with Kalisch (on Genesis) and even Knobel, that the change in Gen. ii. 4 from Elohim to Jehovah-Elohim was made with the design to indicate that the God of creation was the revealed God of the Jews, Jehovah. But the failure of any theory fairly to explain all the cases brings us to the no-theory that while the distinct accounts already in existence may have suggested diverse phraseology, yet, in the main, the choice of the divine names was a matter of unconscious influence, much like the selection of the names of the Saviour, whether Christ Jesus or Jesus Christ.

Now the recognition of such things incorporated in the Pentateuch in no way affects the view that the law-giver, Moses, was directly or indirectly the responsible author of the book —unless it were shown that these embodied documents were certainly later than his time.

And this leads to the remark that the attempts to invalidate the traditional view in regard to the authorship of the Pentateuch may all be characterized as efforts to set aside the usual laws of evidence by evasions and side-issues,—chiefly unwarranted inferences or unfounded assertions. In other words, they steadily divert the attention from the *central* features of the case to a maze of minor discussions, either without bearing on the question or unsupported by satisfactory proof. We are not to be diverted by a labyrinth of petty assumptions and ingenious, but arbitrary, suppositions, from the great decisive features of evidence, which, if they are as old as the hills, are also as firm. The great principles of evidence cannot be set aside.

Now glancing rapidly over this whole field —which is all I can do—when we look at the history of the Pentateuch, we find it coming to us from remote antiquity accredited as substantially the work of Moses, in the same way as ancient classic writers or Josephus—with this remarkable difference, that the books of Moses are embedded in the history and testimony and institutions of a whole nation. Nor had any other authorship ever been thought of.

We find again that, so far as any claim is put forth by the books themselves, it is for this authorship in general. Deuteronomy expressly claims throughout to be Moses' words, and in xxxi. 9, 24-26 the principal part of it (certainly xii.-xxvi.) is declared to have been written by him. In four previous passages in the Pentateuch (Ex. xviii. 14; xxiv. 4; xxxiv.

27; Num. xxxiii. 2) he is declared to have committed certain things to writing. And not only is the law of Leviticus again and again introduced with the statement, "the Lord spake unto Moses," where, too, as Professor Green well says, "the circumstances of these enactments are inseparably united with the historical narrative of the time," but in a dozen places in Deuteronomy the speaker Moses refers to previous enactments of Exodus, Leviticus, Numbers *as given by him*.[9] To which may be added the important fact that the essential and systematic unity of the present Pentateuch as a composition is affirmed by such analysts as Ewald, Tuch, Knobel, Hupfeld, in the strongest terms, and is too obvious to be disputed.

Again, the existence of a book in the hands of the nation, a book called "the law," "the law of Moses," "the book of the law," "the book of the law by the hand of Moses"—all the same—can be traced back—with quotations identifying it—from the New Testament through Esdras, Maccabees, Ecclesiasticus, and, with more or less distinctness, nearly all the several books of the Old Testament up to Joshua.[10] The references of this

[9] Stebbins, "Study of the Pentateuch," pp. 184–6.
[10] Stebbins, *ib.* p. 83.

kind to such a book can be enumerated by the score, and the undoubted quotations from and allusions to its contents, specifically, by the hundred.

Such are the claims and testimonies. And while they certainly do not assert in set terms that every portion of these books was written down by Moses or by his amanuensis, neither is it necessary for us so to affirm. For while we might well stand firm on the position of Schultz, that Moses was both the Jehovist and Deuteronomist, using the older Elohistic records and composing the whole Pentateuch except the concluding part of Deuteronomy (and the glosses that have since crept in), we might, if we chose, hold with Kurtz that the most of Deuteronomy and large portions of the Pentateuch being written by Moses in person, the remainder was arranged and compiled under his direction before entering the promised land; or perhaps we should occupy no unwarrantable position if we held, with Delitzsch formerly, that the completion of the whole work, of which Deuteronomy and much else were by the hand of Moses, was reserved for one or more of his trusted associates, as Eleazer the priest, and Joshua, who was a prophet, or, some one of the elders on whom the spirit of God rested.

With this explanation I proceed to remark succinctly, how the original and unbroken testimony that Moses is responsible for the Pentateuch is confirmed by all the internal indications of which the case naturally admits.

The peculiarities of its archaic diction, exhibiting, at least in parts of it, a marked difference from the later books, except as those quote or refer to this older book, have been too often pointed out in detail, and too forcibly asserted by scholars whose testimony is not to be disputed (such as De Wette, Gesenius, Ewald, Delitzsch,[11]) to require me to go into details here.

In connection with these admitted marks of antiquity—often, if you please, a higher antiquity than the time of the Exodus and Moses—we find the narrative tinged with language that belongs only to the influences and circumstances of a residence in Egypt. The ancient narrative of the deluge incorporates, as given to us, the Egyptian תֵּבָה for the ark. The narrative of Moses' infancy and rescue, has the same word, and three others of Egyp-

---

[11] Thus Delitzsch writes in 1877 ("Preface to the Levitical Priests," p. 10), "The so-called Elohistic language is ancient throughout; there is no trace of the peculiar post-exilic forms and syntax." But this Elohistic portion is that which it is now attempted to place after the exile.

tian origin, together with the Egyptian phrase "the lip of the river." A large number of other words found in the papyri and on the monuments cling to the book, in token of the recent contact of its author with Egypt.

Again, the freshness and minuteness and exactness of correspondence between this narrative and the Egyptian antiquities of the time, is incompatible with any considerable interval between the Exodus and the composition of the Egyptian period of this Hebrew history. And here let me fall back on so great an authority as that of R. S. Poole, deliberately pronounced within three years. After speaking of the "extraordinary acuteness and skill" with which German and Dutch critics have labored upon the Mosaic documents alone, "and their result" "to reduce the date of the documents, except a few fragments, many centuries," he proceeds to say that "the work has been that of great literary critics, not archæologists. The Egyptian documents emphatically call for a reconsideration of the whole question of the date of the Pentateuch. It is now certain that the narrative of the history of Joseph, and the sojourn and exodus of the Israelites, that is to say, the portion from Genesis xxxix. to Exodus xv., so far as it relates to Egypt, is substantially not much later than 1300 B. C. [about the time he assigns for the Exodus], in other words was written while the memory of the events was fresh. The minute accuracy of the text is inconsistent with any later date. It is not merely that it shows knowledge of Egypt, but knowledge of Egypt under the Ramessides and yet earlier. The condition of the country, the chief cities of the frontier, the composition of the army, are true of the age of the Ramessides, and not true of the Pharaohs contemporary with Solomon and his successors." And after a long list of such marked and striking congruities, Mr. Poole proceeds, "These arguments have not failed to strike foreign Egyptologists who have no theological bias. These independent scholars, without actually formulating any view of the date of the greater part of the Pentateuch, appear uniformly to treat its text as an authority to be cited side by side with Egyptian monuments. So Lepsius in his researches on the date of the Exodus, and Brugsch in his discussion of the route, Chabas in his paper on Rameses and Pithom. Of course it would be unfair to implicate any one of these scholars in the inferences expressed above, but at the same time it is impossible that they can, for instance, hold Kuenen's theories of the date of the Pentateuch, so far as the part relating to

Egypt is concerned. They have taken the two sets of documents, Hebrew and Egyptian, side by side, and, in the working of the elaborate problems, found everything consistent with accuracy on both sides; and of course accuracy would not be maintained in a tradition handed down through several centuries."[12]

"If," proceeds the same writer, "the large portion of the Pentateuch relating to the Egyptian period of Hebrew history, including as it does Elohistic as well as Jehovistic sections, is of the remote antiquity here claimed for it, no one can doubt that the first four books are substantially of the same age."

Again, the Pentateuch from the time of the Exodus contains abundant contemporaneous marks of the long wandering. It is sprinkled with arrangements for a migratory nation *on its migrations*. How prominent the legislation for the march in all the details of the march, and for the construction and transportation of the movable tabernacle and for sanitary matters on the way! The minuteness of details of these things, and of the census, and the princes' offerings, is completely in keeping and of necessity as exact directions given to be exactly executed then and there, precisely like some contract with all the specifications to

[12] "Contemporary Review," March, 1879.

build a house—or as facts of contemporaneous interest *only;* but, except as given for direct use and contemporary record, so intolerably tedious, that as a matter of later and distant history it is, as Delitzsch truly remarks, "inconceivable" they should ever have been preserved or invented, much less recorded and transmitted. The wood of which the tabernacle is to be made is the shittim wood, the one prevalent tree of the Sinaitic Wadies, and the only solid tree of sufficient size to furnish the planks as prescribed. The cypress of Palestine is not there, nor the cedar, except in slight quantities for purification,—for a purpose like that for which it was used in Egypt. The game of the wilderness—like the chamois—is included among the clean animals of the Law. Blunt in his "Undesigned Coincidences" has mentioned several minute but almost concealed correspondences in regard to the fall of Korah's company, the arrangement of the tribes with reference to the tabernacle, and the like, which could have come only from a participant in the journey.

Professor W. Robertson Smith does indeed say that "the Pentateuch displays an exact topographical knowledge of Palestine, but by no means so exact a knowledge of the wilderness of wandering. . . . . . . Accordingly, the patriarchal sites can still be set down on the map with definiteness, but geographers are still unable to assign with certainty the site of Mt. Sinai, because the narrative has none of that local color which the story of an eye-witness is sure to possess." But the simple reason for the difference—so far as it exists—is that fixed landmarks, circumstantial differences, and permanent populations have in the one case furnished means of identification, in the other not. The threescore and ten palm trees and twelve wells of water at Elim are local coloring enough. Sinai, we maintain, can be identified by the features indicated in the narrative, probably the wilderness of Sin, and the place of crossing the Red Sea, the encampment by the sea, perhaps Marah, possibly the region of the quails. But as a general thing there *exists*, whether in the Sinaitic peninsula, or still more in the wilderness of wandering, no *local coloring*. It is in the wilderness—as the traveller can testify—a monotonous waste, with no discernible landmarks by which to describe, and, in the peninsula, a maze of *similar* wadies running among rocks, hills and mountains. There is, for the most part, absolutely nothing by which specifically to indicate them, except in the order and time of the journey, and no local population to have handed down the names or knowledge of them in the absence of specified landmarks. The objection misconceives the whole aspect of the case.

Again, a mark of the time of the composition, or the time of Moses, is found in the progressive adaptive legislation incorporated with the more permanent matters. Thus it has often been pointed out how, as emergencies arose on the way, the earlier laws were modified to meet the emergency, by supplementary legislation. Mr. Stebbins affirms that in Deuteronomy there are as many as sixty such amendments or modifications of the laws as given in Exodus and Numbers; besides at least a dozen express references to the previous legislation of Moses. At the time of the last residence at Kadesh, just before the final departure for Canaan, we have some express regulations with reference to their entering that country to settle, and the new circumstances ensuing. Still other regulations or modifications are made when the Israelites had left the wilderness, and were encamped by the Jordan. All bears the mark of the long journey and the shifting exigencies. And, as has been well said, the difference between the hopeful strain in which Moses addresses Israel at the close of the original law-giving (Lev. xxvi.) and the sad, solemn and monitory tone of the reminiscences and exhortations of Deuteronomy, is precisely that which belonged to the different occasions and the man.

Such, briefly indicated in merest outline, are some of the constraining reasons why we believe with the ancient Jewish church, apparently with the Saviour and the apostles, and the whole Christian Church till the present century, that Moses was the responsible author of their ancient records. The reasons seem to us massive and conclusive. They settle the question unless there are insuperable reasons to the contrary. But we cheerfully listen to whatever can be alleged against this mass of evidence. It is precisely the same kind of evidence, be it observed, on which rests the authorship, not of one or some, but all the writings of the past, just as soon as the author and his contemporary generation have passed away, with this mighty difference, that our volume is incorporated, as I have remarked, with the history, literature, institutions and traditions of a great continuous nation from the very beginning, as no other authorship ever has been or can be. Be it remembered that the denial which—unless for the most imperative necessity—rejects the accredited authorship of the Pentateuch, in the same denial is dislodging the foundations of literary history—and is a process to which no limits can be set.

And here—in the objections hitherto urged—we do not seem to find anything which carries constraining force. We admit some difficulties which await solution. But they are no more than are reasonably to be expected, if so many. Some of the objections are assertions that cannot be maintained, others are inferences that do not bind.

Indeed so rapid has been the succession and to some degree so evanescent the force of the objections raised that one hardly knows what of them are still relied upon, so do the fashions change.

The old difficulties raised concerning the art of writing, and from the alleged mistakes of narrative concerning Egyptian customs have long been buried deep out of sight.

The allegation that the relation of a miracle proves the narrative to be a late tradition, rests on the groundless assumption that there can be no miracle.

The difficulty of receiving as the narrative of a participant or contemporary the account of the wandering, because of the impracticability of providing for such a multitude, would indeed be insuperable but for the very circumstances stated in the narrative,—including the miraculous provision.

The objection from the presence of alleged documents in the narrative long managed to hide, under a vast multitude of details and a cloud of mist, the very simple fact that the presence of such documents in no way militated against the final Mosaic authorship—unless these documents contained anachronisms, clear marks of later date.

The attempt to find such anachronisms has proved so feeble as to be fairly pronounced a failure. We have but to concede a few, a very few instances of the slightest revision or of explanatory glosses, such as were easily and naturally incorporated with the text, and all is clear. Indeed the few patches of this kind betray themselves almost at once. Of plausible anachronisms the list is of the scantiest. The case of "Dan" mentioned in Genesis xiv. is the strongest, but is easily explained in several ways, one of which is (with Ewald) that, in keeping with the other explanatory names, this also was inserted and the older name displaced. When Prof. Robertson Smith still insists on the case of "westward and southward"—literally sea-ward and negev-ward—as expressions for this purpose that could only be formed in Palestine, his application of the fact is a *non-sequitur*. They were formed in Palestine, and there they were incorporated with the Hebrew or Palestinian language in which Abraham and afterward Moses found them and used them. A few statements, such as concerning the meekness of Moses, the eating of manna till they came to the borders of Canaan, and the size of an omer, and other similar parenthetical remarks, such as may be conceded to be by a later hand, and of course the account of Moses' death—just as the date of Bradford's death is subjoined to his own manuscript account of the Plymouth Pilgrims and their decease one after another—comprise the main body of these difficulties. The allusion to the kings reigning in Edom before any reigned in Israel, some two similar passages (Lev. xviii. 28, Deut. ii. 12), and a few expressions in Deuteronomy may perhaps be added.

Now making the rather obvious supposition of a few such easy and natural revisions and glosses, and what weight does their presence carry to detract from the great and fundamental aspects of the authorship? Of the numerical or arithmetical objections so carefully collected and so confidently paraded some twenty years ago, may we not as confidently say that they were overwhelmed by an avalanche of effectual refutations, proving in detail an unwarrantable treatment of the narrative by arbitrary and often clearly false limitations or expansions, and in case of real difficulties by the equally arbitrary exclusion of explanations perfectly fair and feasible? Thus much in brief for the case as it has existed until the most recent times.

But what shall be said of the latest form of objection which has arisen after some nineteen years or so—like another lunar cycle? I mean the theory of Kuenen as in part interpreted by Prof. Smith. For a general refutation of that theory as advanced by this bright Scotch Professor, in his main position that the distinctive Priesthood of Aaron's sons and the ritual establishment of Levitical law did not exist before the time of Ezra—I refer you to a discussion in the January number of the "Presbyterian Review" and elsewhere by an honored professor of this Theological Seminary, Dr. Green. And in the demolition of that main position of Robertson Smith, the theory of the master Kuenen is also demolished. And how pretentious is the airy structure in its large preparations and in the perverse ingenuity of its details. It was a bold man who as a preliminary breaking of the ground, undertook to reverse the decision of the great host of his critical predecessors and place the so-called

Jehovist earlier in time than the Elohist; who ventured openly to set up his "supposition with respect to the Mosaic period" and his "conception of historical development," as a test, and on the strength of that supposition remanded the Pentateuch to a later age; who dares to assert that the writers of the books "fearlessly allowed themselves to be guided in their statements by the wants of the present and the requirements of the future," "and considered themselves exempt from all responsibility;" who after ruling out the historical books as unhistorical and as only expressing "*the idea* which was entertained of that history in the eighth century," yet proceeds to build up half a volume of Israel's history out of these very repudiated sources; who, to rid himself of the troublesome witness of Chronicles, could summarily dismiss the Chronicler as one who with all the traditional facts clearly before him yet gave an entirely different version for his priestly ends; who can rest the main weight of his central position on the implied assumption that the violation of a law, even the failure to mention a custom, is evidence that no such law or custom existed; and who can deliberately face all the seeming impossibilities of the allegation that priestly ordinances were made known and imposed upon the Jewish nation now *for the first time* by Ezra, and when modified by Nehemiah or perhaps others, the fraud was quietly palmed off upon the returned exiles as "the laws of God by the hand of Moses"—and so received without a *remonstrance or a suspicion*.

And when reinforced by all the labor and ingenuity of Wellhausen the main features of the case remain unchanged. And, as I believe, it is only a question of a little time for rallying to the defence, and we shall see this airy fabric like its predecessors vanish into thin air again. Already it is clearly shown not only that even on Wellhausen's own ground of natural development, a defined priestly service in connection with the Priesthood would have been at the Exodus prompted by the singular completeness of the then existing priestly functions and religious ceremonies of Egypt itself,[13] but there are historic indications, *inseparable* from the records of the region, that a ritual was established by Moses on the march and that it certainly existed prior to the time of the exile.[14] Furthermore the dictum

[13] Wilkinson's "Ancient Egyptians," i. 259, seq., 311, seq.

[14] See Exodus xxiv. 6; Deut. xxiii. 10; Ps. xcix; See also Deut. xviii. 1, 2, in connection with Numbers xviii. 20, 23; Deuteronomy being, by decision of this school of critics, not later than Josiah's time.

that remonstrances for the non-observance of a law or code prove its non-existence, breaks down wherever it is applied, whether to the morals of Israel in Isaiah and Ezekiel's time, where it would show that the nation had no knowledge even of such fundamental laws as against murder, promiscuous adultery, robbery, fraud, and sin of every kind;[15] and also through most of the history of the New Testament church when it would show that there was no knowledge of law or gospel even on the part of the Roman priesthood. Again, this theory, comprising the position that Moses framed no priestly ordinances and also that David and Solomon composed no psalms nor proverbs, involves the singular improbability that what it terms "the Creative period" (Moses' time) created nothing and that the most active and fruitful periods produced nothing, but that the time of abject depression, general decadence and secondary ability is the grat source of the magnificent Hebrew literature.[16] The theory would still further

[15] Ezekiel xxii. 6–12; xxxiii. 26; Isaiah i. 10, 15, 21, 23, etc.

[16] For this and other important suggestions in this paragraph I am indebted to the elaborate though condensed article of Professor Hermann J. Strack on "The Pentateuch," in the last edition of Herzog's "Real-Encyklopädie." I have thought his article valuable enough to be added

stultify many of the provisions contained in this "priest code," by making them to originate at a time when the occasion for them had passed centuries before. This would apply not alone to the legislation for the march in general, but to such specific directions as those concerning the Urim and Thummim which Aaron was to bear (Ex. xxviii. 29, 30), and which usage was previously extant in the time of Ezra and Nehemiah (Neh. vii. 65; Ezra ii. 63); to the right of booty (Num. xxxi. 21-24); to the original assignment of cities to the Levites (Num. xxxv.); and to the ancient ordinance of the jubilee year, Lev. xxv., involving the relations of these Levites (vs. 32, 33). Indeed the existence of the ritual code not only appears from Deuteronomy (conceded to be older than the exile) with its distinction of clean and unclean (Deut. xii. 15), but some of the permitted food of that code were characteristic animals of the wilderness (xiv. 5). Further yet, the effort to trace the language of the Pentateuchal priestly code to the time of Ezekiel or later, has been vigorously retorted by showing, as in the names of the four chief

(a part of it) as an Appendix to these Lectures. His argument is the more noteworthy because he accepts the now prevalent German theory of four principal documents and one or more redactors.

colors of the priest code, that the language of the former is plainly original and ancient, in contrast to the Aramean and Arian forms of the time of the Chronicles.[17] And to crown all the other inconsistencies of the theory comes the pervasive moral monstrosity of a scheme which would assign to Ezra and Nehemiah a concerted[18] and successful plan to palm off upon Israel a complexus of impostures extending from Exodus to Kings and Chronicles; —the story of Moses' birth being but a myth,[19] the story of the Law-giving at Sinai, "the product of a poetic necessity," that mountain being but the Olympus of the Hebrews, and the process of centuries "being condensed into a single thrilling moment for the sake of a vivid impression,"[20] the Decalogue belonging perhaps to the time of Manasseh, Deuteronomy a fabrication of the seventh century, all the historic setting of the Mosaic legislation a series of supplementary, carefully adjusted traditions made by the scribes so as to advance "with all the progressive requirements of life"; Judges a "systematic generalization, contradicted by facts which we otherwise know"[21]; Chronicles written to sustain

[17] See this argument in Delitzsch's Preface to "The Levitical Priests," p. 11, seq.
[18] Wellhausen, "Encyc. Brit." xiii. 418.
[19] *Ib.* p. 399.   [20] *Ib.* p. 400.   [21] *Ib.* p. 400.

the imposition, and Kings skilfully interpreted and modified by these same ingenious and unscrupulous men for the same purpose.

Add to all this that Ezra and Nehemiah themselves, who are put forward as the chief fabricators of this alleged new Levitical code, present themselves in no such attitude, but as restorers of the ancient service. Ezra comes forward simply as "a ready scribe in *the law of Moses* which the Lord God of Israel had given" (Ez. vii. 6, 11) who "had prepared his heart to seek the law of the Lord and do it." And when he read the law publicly to the people, it was "the book of the law of Moses, which the Lord had commanded Israel" (Neh. viii. 1), "The law which the Lord had commanded Moses" (verse 14) with specific references to the priest code of Leviticus (viii. 9, comp. Lev. xxiii. 24; also Neh. viii. 14, 15, 18, comp. Lev. xxiii. 40, 42, 36). And both Ezra and Nehemiah make it the burden of their confessions that "from the days of their fathers the people had been in a great trespass and cast God's law behind their backs" (Ez. ix. 6, 7, 10, Neh. ix. 26, 28, 29, 30, 34). Yet these are the men who are declared to be the originators of the Levitical code, and this is the mountainous series of elaborate and systematic and monstrous impostures that we are expected to receive on such shallow and self-conflicting arguments as have been indicated. Surely when such a structure as this goes down, we can hardly say "great was the fall of it"; for however ingenious, not great was the structure.

And now, gentlemen, I have completed the pleasant task I have undertaken,—to set before you in some degree the five books of Moses as containing the sources of history. It has been with me a labor of interest and love to which I would have been glad to devote more time and labor were it consistent with other engagements. I have wished in these days of cavil to emphasize the fact that not only is our ancient Pentateuch not a book to be ashamed of, but it is a book to glory in, —with its wonderful elucidations of the whole early condition of our globe and of our race, with its own announcement of the most momentous events and the most vital institutions, its clear unfolding of the germs of all subsequent life, and its graphic delineations of scenes and persons otherwise shrouded in mist or hidden behind an impenetrable veil. It is the grandest of histories, the noblest series of biographies, the divine germ of all human institutions, the substructure of all religious hopes, and the primal clue to all the past and the future of our race. My discussion has, from its limits, necessarily been suggestive, rather than exhaustive. But should I have made any suggestion fruitful of better results in any of your minds, if I have even prompted you to some fresh inquiries along any portion of this broad and fruitful field, or stimulated any of you to broader investigations or a profounder sacred scholarship, my best wishes will have been accomplished. And though my discussion has dealt largely with the secondary aspect of the volume, it has not been in disparagement, but in support, of its primary ends. And I cannot in closing better express my views on this point than in the words of a brilliant expositor:

"The Torah is the basis of the Old Testament, and the Old Testament the preparation for the religion of Redemption. What the four gospels are to the New Testament, that are the five books of the law to the Old Testament. But not merely do beginning and beginning, but beginning and end of the Old and New Testament canon, Genesis and Apocalypse, run together like the ends of a circle. The creation of the heavens and earth on the first pages of Genesis corresponds to the creation of the new heavens and the new earth on the last page of Revelation. To the first creation which had Adam for its end, corresponds the new creation which takes the second Adam for its beginning. Thus does the Holy Scripture form a unity compacted into itself, to show that not alone this or that book, but the whole is a work of the Holy Spirit. The Torah, with its shadow of good things to come, is the root, the Apocalypse, penetrating into the 'world to come,' is the top. Take away the three first chapters of Genesis from the Bible, and you take away the *terminus a quo;* take away the last three chapters of the Apocalypse, and you take away the terminus *ad quem*." And now, with many thanks for your kind attention, I take my leave.

APPENDIX.

STRACK ON THE PENTATEUCH.

The following extract contains the more important part of Prof. Hermann L. Strack's article on the Pentateuch, in the last edition of Herzog's "Real-Encyklopädie," Leipzig, 1882. His criticisms on the theory of Wellhausen, which close the extract, would not be sufficiently intelligible without his account of the recent theories, which precedes it. We omit his summary of the contents of the Pentateuch, his "justification of the Criticism," and his brief narrative of its history from the time of Astruc till recent times—the latter topic being by this time somewhat familiar. Strack's criticisms are the more significant, because of his complete sympathy with the "Higher Criticism." He would find the unity of compilation rather in the Hexateuch (including Joshua) than the Pentateuch. He classifies the principal theories as three: the Fragment, Supplement, and Document theories. He expresses his sympathy with the third, within the range of which, he says, "there exist considerable differences of opinion, relating less to the analysis than to the order and age of the sources."[1]

He recounts the several names that have been given to these documents thus: *a*. The first Elohist, the Ground-writing, Book of Origins, Analytic Narrator, A., and (by Wellhausen) P. C. (and 2). *b*. The second Elohist, the younger Elohist, the third Narrator, the Theocratic Narrator, B. or North-Israelitish Narrator, C., and (Wellhausen) E. *c*. The Jehovist, Supplementer, Fourth Narrator, Prophetic Narrator, C., and (Wellhausen) J. *d*. Deuteronomist, D.

Strack prefers Wellhausen's designation as least objectionable, using, however, P. instead of P. C. (priest code) and E.[2] instead of E. His

[1] He affirms (as against Keil) that "Critics of all tendencies (Delitzsch, Wellhausen, etc.) are agreed upon the necessity of a separation of the fundamental documents, and, secondly, that in the analysis of very many sections unanimity has been gained, either complete or in the main. Thus in the first nine chapters of Genesis, Nöldeke, Dillmann and Wellhausen unanimously refer to the so-called Elohist, i.–ii. 3a; v. (except ver. 29); vi. 9–22; vii. 11, 13–16a, 18–21, 24; viii. 1, 2a; 3b–5, 13a, 14–19; ix. 1–17. Differences exist in reference to five verses or parts of verses. Nöldeke and Dillmann add vii. 6; Nöldeke adds vii. 22, where Dillmann assumes an interference by the compiler (redactor), and Wellhausen is for rejection; vii. 23 is rejected by Nöldeke and Wellhausen, while Dillmann refers the second half-verse, but not with full confidence, to the same document; of the first of the two half-verses, viii. 3a, 13b, which Wellhausen adds, Dillmann only says it is 'probably' by the Jehovist." It will be observed that the claim is cautious—for "very many sections," and that the specification made is carefully chosen.

subsequent statements, which we give, will show the latest phases of the discussion, the fluctuations and caprices of the theories, and the insurmountable objections to the latest, most elaborate, and most ingenious of them. His blows are the more telling because of his sympathy with the "critical" process. He proceeds as follows:

THE MOST IMPORTANT OPINIONS AT PRESENT ADVOCATED.

a. Eb. Schrader, in the eighth edition of De Wette's "Introduction to the Old Testament" (Berlin, 1869), declares for a union of the Document and Supplement theories; holding that P., recognizable until the end of the book of Joshua, wrote in the beginning of David's reign, was most certainly a priest, probably a Judean; that E.[2], traceable to I Kings ix. 28, probably a North-Israelite, wrote soon after the separation of the kingdoms, between 975 and 950; that probably both made use of written materials; that J., also belonging to the northern kingdom, between 825 and 800, combined in a free way the works of P. and E.[2] into a harmonious whole, making many additions, partly from other written records (*e. g.*, Ex. xxi.–xxiii.), partly from oral traditions. The groundwork of Deuteronomy (iv. 44 to chap xxviii.) was composed not long before the eighteenth year of Josiah by some one intimately related to Jeremiah, an inspired man, who, after the destruction of the kingdom of Judah, inserted his work into P., E.[2], J. The separation of the Thora, *i. e.*, of the Pentateuch in its present form, from the subsequent history, did not take place before the end of the Babylonian captivity. It was publicly sanctioned at the time of Ezra. Schrader even now holds fast to his theory.

b. Th. Nöldeke, in his investigations upon the criticism of the Old Testament, proposed the following view: P., E.², J. spring from the tenth century, or before the ninth. E.² is extant only in J.'s recasting. P. may not be the oldest writing, but cannot be much younger than the two others. The author of the part D., written shortly before the reformation of Josiah, wrought his work into the previously complete Haxateuch, perhaps also separated the book of Joshua. From information given me on the 20th of May, 1882, in regard to Nöldeke's present position on the Pentateuch criticism, I infer the following: Nöldeke has given up his attempt at identifying the editor (redactor) with the writer of Deuteronomy. He declares it impossible to separate critically the mass of the Pentateuch which remains after P. and D. are withdrawn from it. He cannot accede to the opinion of Graf and Wellhausen. In the law literature no rectilinear development can be recognized. He adheres to the dependence of Ezekiel upon P. The writer of Deuteronomy must at all events have had before him a law literature written in essentially the same style and often in the same phraseology as that of the priest code.

c. Aug. Dillmann will express his opinion consecutively at the end of his revision of Knobel's "Commentary on the Hexateuch." From his present utterances we may infer the following: Whether P. or E.^{2} may claim priority of date is a question. E.^{2}, belonging to the bloom of the prophetic life in the central tribes, is certainly older than J., whose writing rests upon that of E.^{2} throughout, and is much more nearly related to D. in time and spirit, the latter having been composed shortly before Josiah's reform. P., E.^{2}, and J. were wrought together by one editor (before or after D.?). The narrative of Nehemiah, viii.–x., has reference to the whole Pentateuch.—For traces of post-exile revision and editing, see "Comm. on Ex. and Lev.," pp. viii., 356 *ff.*, 620.—P., E.^{2}, and J. have very ancient sources, especially the legal contents; *e. g.*, E. has received the Book of the Covenant, Ex. xx., xxii. to xxiii. 19; P. and J., in Lev. v. 1–6, 21, 26 (compare vi., vii. 17–26), make use of an older codex ("Law of Sinai").

d. 1. Franz Delitzsch wrote as late as 1872, (Com. on Gen.), "The book of Deuteronomy shows itself Mosaic, and must in the main be recognized as Mosaic;" and "A man like Eleazar the priest wrote the great work beginning with בראשית ברא into which he put the covenant. A second, like Joshua, who is a prophet and spoke like a prophet or one of those זקנים upon whom the spirit of Moses rested, found himself empowered to complete this work, and he embodied with it the entire Deuteronomy, by which he had formed himself. Thus originated the Thora, not without the use of other written documents by both narrators." Since 1876 Delitzsch, at first especially influenced by Aug. Kayser, has modified his views considerably, and in such a manner that he has approached Graf and his disciples as to the succession and analysis of the original writings; but has quite differently determined the time of their production, and has earnestly declared himself against the conclusions which that school draws in regard to the history, especially the religious history of Israel, as the result of their critical investigations. Concerning E.², I find in Delitzsch's writings only the following expression (Pent.-Crit. Stud., 1880, P. 338, f.)—"It is probable that the book of the covenant, the laws of the two tables and various narrations, belonging to the so-called second Elohist, were already interwoven with the Jehovistic work when Deuteronomy originated and became attached to it." Next in order Delitzsch places J. D is ranked after Solomon, but before Isaiah. Next is the law of sanctification, *i. e.*, especially the code contained in Lev. xvii.–xxvi. Then comes P., the youngest figure in the Legislation that refers back to Moses, written before the exile, and before Ezekiel. Delitzsch cites by way of comparison the many records previous to the Canonical Gospels, and adds that "he is now firmly convinced that the process of origin and growth by which the Thora attained its final form, extends down to the post-exilic epoch, and perhaps had not been perfected at the time when the Samaritan Pentateuch and the Greek translation came into existence. So much the more firmly do we take our stand upon the Mosaic origin and revealed character of its (the Thora's) basis."

e. J. Wellhausen's views: Even the Decalogue is not Mosaic. The covenant book, Ex. xx. 22 to ch. xxiii. 19, is "given to a people stationary and perfectly accustomed to an agricultural life." J. belongs "to the golden period of Hebrew literature, the time of the kings and prophets, preceding the destruction of both Israelitish kingdoms by the Assyrians." "It is worthy of note that after the blessing of Balaam, J. suddenly breaks off. Only in Num. xxv. 1–5 and Deut. xxxiv. one might be inclined to find some trace of this noble historic work, e. g., xxxiv, 7b." $E.^2$ shows us a more progressive and fundamental religiousness, and treats also of the subjugation of Canaan. "Both sources have perhaps undergone several enlarged editions and are combined not as $J.^1$ and $E.^2$ but as $J.^3$ and $E.^3$" D. composed shortly before the eighteenth year of Josiah and at that time containing only chapters xii.–xxvi., underwent, "not before the exile," two enlarged editions independent of one another. The union of the two editions and the insertion of the work thus composed into J. $E.^2$ took place perhaps in immediate connection with the work on Deuteronomy by which J. and $E.^2$ were blended into J. $E.^2$ Lev. xvii.–xxvi., is a collection of laws which originated in the exile, between Ezekiel and the priest code, but nearer Ezekiel, although not composed by him. It was embodied into P. in a suitable form. The part of the Hexateuch remaining after the separation of J. E.² and D. is later than the exile, "does not bear the character of strict unity," but is " a conglomerate, as it were, of the work of an entire school." Around a fundamental germ, Q., which was remarkable for its historic system, there have sprung up (irrespective of earlier additions) "a number of secondary and tertiary growths which in form do not belong to it, but in material are perfectly homogeneous; so that the whole may be regarded, not as a literary, but as an historic unity." The legislation of the middle books (Ex. xxv.–xxxi., xxxv.–xl., Lev., Num. i.–x., xv.–xix., xxv.–xxxvi., with insignificant exceptions); standing in closest relations with Q. in language and contents, as well as by direct references, is designated as a priest-code. As originally belonging to Q. are proven only: Ex. xxv.–xxix., Lev. ix., x. 1–5, 12–15; ch. xvi. Num. i. 1–16. i. 48 to ch. iii., ix. 15 to ch. x. 28; chs. xvi. partly, xvii., xviii., xxv., 6–19; xxvi. xxvii., xxxii., partly, xxxiii. 50 to ch. xxxvi. This legislative and historical work, already inserted into J. E.² D., was published and introduced by Ezra in the year 444; "for there is no doubt that the law of Ezra was the entire Pentateuch."

f. K. H. Graf, although he died July 16, 1869, must be mentioned here on account of the great influence which his main theory has exerted and still exerts. He declared on the basis of his investigations into the history of the cultus, that the central legislation of the Pentateuch bore the most unmistakable traces of a composition after the exile. The objections of Nöldeke and Riehm convinced Graf that the fundamental writing (Grundschrift) could not be divided in such a manner. The result was, not that he withdrew his assertion, but in a brief essay composed shortly before his death, he declared that the whole so-called fundamental writing was the product of an age after the exile; that J. was composed in the middle of the eighth century, or about the time of Ahaz; D. shortly before the eighteenth year of Josiah; the Deuteronomist (Inserter of D.), in the first half of the exile; P., after the exile, introduced by Ezra; insertion in J. D. soon after Ezra.

g. Ed. Reuss says: "The Decalogue is perhaps the very oldest piece of the written legislation, but is not Mosaic." The covenant book belongs presumably to the time of Jehoshaphat (See 2 Chron. xvii. 7); the so-called second decalogue, Ex. xxxiv. 11 ff. is very near it in time; J., the book of sacred history, embracing the fulfilment of the promises by the possession of the promised land, composed by an Israelite of the ten tribes in the second half of the ninth century, before the destruction of the Ephraimite kingdom, has at a later period been so wrought together with the perhaps older E.[2] that a "separation is almost impossible." In the eighteenth year of Josiah was brought to light

D. "an alleged discovery of the priests." It had been written immediately before this, with the purpose of prescribing and establishing as state law, "the fundamental principles of the theocratic constitution." It consisted of Deuteronomy v.-xxvi., xxviii. Between the first captivity and the destruction of the state, D. was joined to J. E.², but not by the writer of D. The section Lev. xvii.-xxvi. is not preserved in its ancient form, but is interwoven with newer parts. The fundamental part is younger than D., written after the time of Ezekiel but before that of Ezra. The work promulgated by Ezra in the year 444 was not the entire Pentateuch, and was not brought finished from Babylon by Ezra, but was written between 458 and 444. The historic frame-work of this composition, "a bare fiction" .... "dreams of an impoverished race," was written by one hand; the principal contents, however, are "a collection of laws from different sources." In the time between Nehemiah and Alexander, the code of Ezra, a number of special laws, and J. E.² D. were joined to form one whole, with little skill and less historic sense, inasmuch as the principle was followed that nothing essential which was then in existence should be lost. "The prophets are to be recognized as older than the law and the psalms as younger than both."

A discussion of all the preceding characteristic views is of course impossible in this place. We will give here, at first, a few general remarks;

then, a condensed discussion upon the methods of treating the problems of Pentateuch criticism which in their time have excited most attention; and finally some observations upon the composition of the Hexateuch, especially the views of Wellhausen and Schrader.

GENERAL DETERMINING PRINCIPLES.

a. Criticism must employ upon the Old Testament essentially the same means and methods as upon other productions of literature. Miracles and prophecies, however, must not of themselves be turned against the Old Testament to disprove its authenticity and genuineness. Criticism operates too much with the theory of *raticinium post eventum* and of the incredibility of miracles. The specific difference of the religion of the Old Testament, its character as revelation, stands firmly fixed in our belief; therefore we will not demand that the rule of natural rectilinear development shall extend over all the history of Israel.

b. Great precaution is necessary in drawing arguments from the linguistic traits of a book or section of the Old Testament. In the first place, the old Hebrew literature preserved to us, is but of small extent. In the second place, copyists often unintentionally, no doubt, substituted for the archaisms and other obscurities, expressions which seemed to them more natural and clear. (For analogies compare the new edition of Luther's Bible with the original publication). Thirdly: Upon the whole we may be justified in pronouncing from diversity of style upon a difference of authorship rather than of time. Fourthly: Even if we find truth in the opinion that "The Hebrew language is incapable of presenting one and the same thought in various forms as most European languages can do; that it is too restricted for this, is too clumsy in style; that when the thought has once found a correct expression any change of form is by the spirit of the language prohibited; and it then passes as current coin": yet we cannot well deny the possibility that the language of an author of special spiritual force might vary at different epochs and in different circumstances.

c. A written code of law, especially a rather extensive one, may exist for a long time without having a universal canonical acceptation, and without being known beyond more or less narrow circles.

d. If it is shown that an account or a statement has been committed to writing in relatively late time, we need not necessarily conclude that the essential part of it had not been correctly handed down or understood. Oral tradition has been of value not to Talmudic Judaism for the first time. Such laws especially as have reference not so much to the people as to the priesthood, may have been preserved within the latter for a long time by tradition.—More depends upon the credibility of what is declared in the Pentateuch concerning history and legislation, than upon the question how much of it Moses wrote.

e. In regard to the conclusions which are drawn from the separate documents as to the character of these documents, we must bear in mind that each redactor has chosen out of the different sources what was best adapted to his own purposes, so that between the complete accounts there has often been either no contradiction, or at least much less than exists now when we compare the incomplete accounts. Here we must mention, too, that criticism, in its separation of documents, in many places depends entirely or essentially upon the conception which it has formed of the character of individual documents, on the basis of other verses and sections which had been already separated on account of their linguistic qualities.

f. Many differences in the legal portions of the Pentateuch are avoided by observing the principle: *Distinque tempora.* One must discriminate whether a law regards the time of Israel's sojourn in the desert or its settlement in Canaan.

THE VIEW OF GRAF AND WELLHAUSEN.

a. The views of scholars as to the origin of the Pentateuch, as the above comparison has shown, differ in very many points. All differences, however, are of little moment when compared with the great opposition which Graf, Aug. Kayser, Reuss, Wellhausen and others have carried into the ranks of the investigators. Up to this time P. was regarded as the oldest original writing, or at least one of the oldest, and was considered as credible at least in its principal points. Up to this time the view was prevalent that the Pentateuch, either in its present form or its separate original writings, had been completed before the exile. The latest school admits that, of extant written laws, the covenant-book alone existed in ancient times; then come the purely historical works E.² and J. (or J. and E.² or J. E.²); thereupon D. follows, as first comprehensive law code; then Ezekiel's Thora, Ez. xl.-xlviii. then the law of sanctification, and last of all P. Wellhausen and others think that the Pentateuch was completed in the year 444; according to Graf, Kayser and Reuss only P., or even only the principal part of P. was sanctioned in the above year.

The wide sweep of this arrangement becomes apparent when we consider how wholly different from all previous notions, the course of Israelitish history is presented by using the results of the Graf-Wellhausen criticism. Here we will give some intimations of this new drift, on the basis of Wellhausen's spirited "History of Israel."

1. The place of worship. The historical and prophetical books afford no trace of an exclusively authorized sanctuary for Hebrew antiquity. The denunciations of the prophets are not directed against the places of worship or their number, but against the false estimate of worship and the abuses connected with it, (p. 23). The Jehovist J. E.² sanctions the plurality of altars. The destruction of Samaria favored efforts at centralization. D. demands local unity of worship, P. presupposes it and transfers it to antiquity by means

of the tabernacle of the covenant, which as a central sanctuary and as a depositary for the ark can nowhere be found in historical tradition.

2. The sacrifices. According to J. E.[2], sacrifice is an ante-Mosaic custom; according to P. it is not. According to J. E.[2] with whom the historical and prophetical books harmonize, the important question concerns the person; according to P. the technicalities of the sacrifice, as well as the when, where, and by whom, and also especially the how (p. 53). P. introduces the sin-offering and the expiatory sacrifice, of which no trace can be found in the Old Testament before Ezekiel (p. 75). By the centralization of worship at Jerusalem, the harmony of sacrifice with the natural occurrences of life was destroyed, and sacrifices had lost their original character.

3. The same thing occurred with reference to the festivals which originally celebrated the beginning (Easter) and the end (Pentecost) of harvest, and the grape gathering, (Autumn). P., moreover, increases the number of festivals by the great day of atonement which took its origin from the fast-days of the exile (p. 113). The Sabbath year, too, and the year of jubilee were not added until late, *i. e.*, in the collection of laws received and compiled by P. (Lev. xvii.–xxvi.)

4. Priests and Levites. In the oldest period of Israel's history we do not find the distinction between priests and laymen. Every one is allowed to kill and sacrifice; priests by calling officiate only at greater religious services. Accord-

ingly we find in the oldest parts of J. E.[2] no mention of priests, no Aaron with Moses. In hoary antiquity there was once a tribe Levi, but it had already disappeared in the time of the judges. Later on Levi is the official name of the members of the priestly families; and out of the Levites grew a spiritual tribe or rather a caste by the name of Levi collectively, which hereditary priesthood, according to the representation of the later writers, from the time of D. already existed in the beginning of Israelitish history.

According to Ezekiel xliv. only the Levites of Jerusalem, the sons of Zadoc, are to remain priests in the new Jerusalem; the other Levites are to be degraded into their servants, and stripped of their priestly rights. According to P. the Levites have never had the right of priesthood, but only the sons of Aaron, who correspond to the sons of Zadoc. The keystone of the sacred edifice which P. erects, is the high priest. A figure of such incomparable importance is a stranger to the remainder of the Old Testament. The existence of a theocratic King by his side cannot be conceived.

5. The inherited rights of the clergy. In antiquity the sacrifices were holy meals, to which priests also were invited if perchance any one of them were present. The owner of a sanctuary employed priests for hire, but these had no legal claims to certain fixed portions of meat. D. already makes some demand of this nature (xviii.

3); P. demands much more (vii. 34). The things set apart become legal income to the priests, and, in addition, are doubled. The forty-eight Levite towns are a fiction, for which the starting-point lies perhaps in the conception of the future Israel imagined by Ezekiel.

A CRITICISM OF THESE THEORIES.

We will now give some contributions to a correct estimate of this newest phase of Pentateuch criticism. A portion of the remarks following can perhaps be applied to other views also.

a. The Egyptians had in very early times a rich literature, and were a people greatly addicted to writing. The Jews were always susceptible to the influence of foreigners. Must they not have begun to note down many things already in Egypt? Would not especially Moses, the adopted son of Pharaoh's daughter, the man educated in all the wisdom of the Egyptians, have described the great deeds which God did through him?

b. Egypt had a numerous and influential caste of priests of different orders, dating from antiquity. So too Israel may be supposed to have possessed a priesthood early, and not to have remained a thousand years without written laws for its priests. We may very well assume that the priest Moses gave directions for a ritual (Ex. xxiv. 6 ff.; Deut. xxxiii. 10; Ps. xcix. 6). There is no want, indeed, of testimonies to the early existence of a priestly, that is, a ritualistic, Thora, which is recognized, not for the first time after the exile. Deut. xxxiii. 10; Micah iii. 11; Jer. xviii. 18; Ez. vii. 26; Zeph. iii. 4; Hosea iii. 4, show that there was a copious written Thora of this kind (Bredenkamp, "Law and Prophets," pp. 36–40). Especially Deuteronomy, which, whenever it may have been composed, was at any rate in existence in the eighteenth year of Josiah, is rich in passages testifying to this fact. Comp. Deut. xviii. 2 (כאשר דבר לו) with Numbers xviii., xx., xxiii. ff.; further, Deuteronomy xxiv. 8, where in כאשר צִוִּיתִם there is a reference to a priestly Thora upon leprosy, such a one as lies before us in Lev. xiii. 14. "Wherever Deuteronomy contents itself with a general outline and sketch of precepts which demand special or additional rules for practice, we may conclude that the more special rules were already in existence which it presupposes and to which it refers" (Delitzsch).

c. The new theory leaves the fundamental periods of Israel's history without literature; no laws or historical records of Moses, no psalms of David, no proverbs of Solomon.

d. The fact that we find in the books after the exile more numerous and exact references to the Pentateuch and its original writings than in those before the exile, is to be accounted for by the fact that with Ezra begins an entirely new period, that of the scribes. In the circumstance that in the entire prophetic literature there is wanting a demand even for inner holiness, there lies "a grave admonition to deal cautiously with the non-appearance of certain thoughts in particular books," as Baudissin once well remarked.

e. The theory of Graf and Wellhausen not only supplants God as a factor in the history of Israel, but must often have recourse abundantly to the very precarious assumption of the presence of fictions.

f. A main reliance of the representatives of the newest school is a conclusion to the non-existence of a certain law from the neglect of its observance. This conclusion, however, by no means carries absolute weight of conviction. Comp. *e. g.*, Jer. xvi. 6 with Deut. xiv. 1. When we reflect upon the corruption of the priests, whose essential duty was to teach (complaints of the prophets, *e. g.*, Jer. xxvii. 7 ff.; Micah iii. 11; Zeph. iii. 4; Isa. often) we shall quite readily perceive that "the transmitted laws remained lying in the temple's archives, instead of governing the life of the people" (Bredenkamp, p. 200).

g. Partly from a critical, partly from an exegetical, point of view, the writings of the Old Testament often experience violent treatment to make them harmonize with the recent construction of history. In proof of this a few examples are enough.

α. Pentateuch. The book of covenant, Exodus xx., xxiv., xxv., according to Wellhausen ("Hist," p. 30 ff.) sanctions the liberty to sacrifice everywhere. The command בכל־המקום אשר אזכיר את־שמי he satisfies himself to explain thus: "That means nothing more than that they did not like (!) to consider a spot where the intercourse between heaven and earth took place as a spot arbitrarily chosen, but regarded it as somehow (!) selected by Deity itself for this service." The actual truth is that this passage forbids to choose the place of sacrifice according to mere human choice; and that it does not indeed exclude a plurality of authorized places of sacrifice at the same time, while it neither presupposes nor demands them. And the command, likewise contained in the covenant book, to appear three times annually before Jehovah (Ex. xxiii. 17) certainly points decisively to a centralization. Compare Delitzsch, "Stud.," 1880, pp. 64, 341, 562, f.; Bredenkamp, pp. 129, 139. With Wellhausen's conclusions from Deuteronomy xxxiii. 8–11, pp. 138–140, compare Bredenkamp, pp. 173–180.

β. According to Wellhausen, the historical books have undergone numerous revisions and reconstructions, by which ideas of later times were always introduced . . . . "retouches to explain and to obviate difficulties. The whole ancient tradition is covered with these as with a Judaistic digestive-fluid," (p. 290). The whole historic treatment in the book of Kings is a pious *Pragmatik*, historically inadmissible, (p. 136). On p. 299 we read that "In Kings from time to time a new prophet is put forward who utters himself in the spirit of D. and the language of Jeremiah and Ezekiel, and then disappears;" and on p. 302, "The anonymous prophets, i. 20, who are all afterwards collectively inserted for the purpose of a detailed *vaticinium ex eventu*, because Israelitish history is never complete without this appendage." A particularly unfavorable judgment is passed upon Chronicles: *e. g.*, p. 219, "Where the chronicles run parallel with the other canonico-historical books, they contain no enrichment, but merely a coloring of tradition through time-serving-motives," p. 631. "Therefore in Chronicles there can be no mention of a tradition from before the exile"; p. 129, "Artificial Genealogies." More favorable and yet critical is Dillmann's view of Chronicles in this encyclopædia (III., pp. 223, 224). The narration Neh. viii.–x. is wrongly interpreted to mean that in the year 444, the Pentateuch, till then unknown, was published and solemnly introduced by Ezra. (Thus Wellhausen, Graf and others.) The picture which the entire tradition beginning with the book Ezra–Nehemiah gives us of Ezra, does not harmonize with the picture drawn by the modern Pentateuch criticism. (Cf. Delitzsch's "Papers for Lutheran Theology," XXXVIII., 1877, pp. 445–50.) In order to set aside a proof for the hereditariness of the priesthood among the descendants of Aaron, Wellhausen must falsely conclude from 1 Sam. ii. 27 ff. that "Zadoc was the founder of an absolutely new line"; he is permitted to be neither priest nor even Levite; the divine threat, however, is not directed against Eli's entire father's house but only against his own family. Wellhausen says (p. 26), "Hezekiah is said even then to have made an attempt to abolish the places of sacrifice outside of Jerusalem, which however passed by without leaving any traces, and is therefore of a doubtful character." But according to p. 28 the reformation of Josiah would hardly have pervaded the people had it not been for the exile following; therefore, even according to Wellhausen, want of success furnishes no cause for doubt.

γ. The prophets. Here too the criticism is not wanting in procedures which are at least hazardous. Thus ברא, Amos iv. 13, Jer. iv. 5, is said not to be originally there (Wellh. p. 349). Joel is regarded by almost all the followers of the Graf-hypothesis as a post-exile writer, etc. The cases of exegetical violence are numerous and important. They fail to see that law and prophecy have two entirely different purposes. The difference between the priest code and the prophets is swelled out into an irreconcilable contradiction. They do not regard the moral character of the ritual law, do not consider that P. knows only of a sin and trespass-offering for those transgressions known as sins of weakness (Cf. Bredenkamp, p. 56, 57). The prophets do not oppose a lawful manner of sacrifice but the practice of the people. Bredenkamp rightly demands that a discrimination should be made between the utterances of the prophets of the northern kingdom and those of the kingdom of Juda on account of their difference of circumstances: In the northern kingdom the warfare is waged more against what is heathenish in worship; in the southern against what is but the outward form of worship. On the passages in the prophets against the sacrifices, compare K. Marti's "Yearbooks for Prot. Theol.," VI., 1880, pp. 308-323; upon Amos v. 21-27 see Bredenkamp, pp. 83-90; upon Jer. vii. 21 ff. id., 108-112. Although not a consideration convincing to every one, yet it deserves to be mentioned that by this modern criticism upon P., God is brought into contradiction with himself: what the older prophets condemned, became after the exile Israel's law and the basis of the later discourses of the prophets.

δ. The Poetical Books. The book of Job is declared to have been written after the time of Jeremiah, e. g., by Wellhausen, acc. to Bleek, Intr. p. 543, note. W. Robt. Smith Old Test. 381. Certainly Job i. 5 does not suit the new construction of the history of sacrifices. Wellhausen's judgment upon the psalms (among other places in p. 507, note) is this: "The question is, not whether there were any psalms written after the exile, but whether there were any written before it." If Psalm xl. 7 ("Sacrifice and offering thou didst not desire") was written before the exile then the sin-offering was mentioned even before Ezekiel (against Wellhausen, p. 75, and Smend on Ezek. xl. 39); but if—what we do not believe—the Psalm was written after the exile, the quite similar utterances, Amos v., Jer. vii., do not exclude the existence of a law of sacrifices at an earlier period. Comp. Bredenk., pp. 59-63, or W. H. Green, Presbyt. Rev. 1882, Jan. No., 142-3.

h. The addition of the priest code. P. contains

a series of laws which after the exile were aimless and impracticable. Urim and Thummim, Ex. xxviii. 30; Lev. viii. 8; Num. xxvii. 21. Comp. Ezra ii. 63; Neh. vii. 65. Year of jubilee, Lev. xxv. 8 ff. Levite towns, Num. xxxv. 1 ff. Law of booty. Num. xxxi. 25 ff. In P. are designated those services only, which the Levites were to render during their journey through the desert; for their residence in the holy land no express provision was made. Such a fiction, as Bredenkamp has already observed, would be most wonderful.

Quite a lively discussion is now carried on concerning the relation of P, especially the law of sanctification, to Ezekiel (H. G., Dillmann's S.) Careful comparison of philological usage shows that Ezekiel is dependent upon H. G. and P, and not the contrary; Compare the references of D. Hoffmann, Magazine for Judaistic Science (1879, 210–215), which Smend in his Comm. upon Ezek. p. xxv.–xxviii. has not noticed, perhaps has not been able to notice. Essential differences exist between Ezekiel and P. *E. g.* Ezek. (xl. 18 ff.) appoints numbers and kinds of sacrifices for the several days of the year quite different from P. (See Smend's Tables, p. 377). A priest might perhaps change the wording of the law; but it is inconceivable that any one, after the time of Ezekiel, and especially in a period which clings entirely to the written word, could introduce, without encountering the slightest opposition, a new unknown, anonymous production, essentially diverging from the law of the prophets which claimed divine authority. Especial weight is laid upon the assertion that D. recognized no difference between priests and Levites; that all Levites were authorized to officiate as priests; that in Ezek. xliv. 5 ff. the degradation of the Levites to be temple-servants and the right of the descendants of Zadoc only to the priesthood were enjoined; that P. presupposed the injunction of Ezek. always to have existed, in which only the venerable ancient name (sons of Aaron) was put in place of the historical name (sons of Zadoc), in order to keep up the appearance of the Mosaic time, (Wellh. p. 128). But the assertion is a false one, that Ezekiel was the first who made any difference between priests and Levites. With Zerubbabel and Joshua there returned (acc. to Ezra ii. 36 ff.; Neh. vii. 43) 4289 priests but only 341 (Neh. 360) Levites; a number of Levites so small certainly not because they feared the degradation threatened by Ezekiel, but because the position of the Levites even before the exile had been a subordinate one. From Ezra ii. 63 we see that the possession of the full right of priesthood was rigidly connected with the proved fact of belonging to the priestly tribe. Ezekiel himself presupposes the difference between priest and Levite as self-evident, xl. 45 ff.; xlii. 13; xliii. 19.

We can conclusively show that many laws of the priest code are older than Deuteronomy. The assertion that the command (Lev. xvii. 1 ff), to sacrifice at the ark of the covenant only, is postdeuteronomic, or indeed post-exilic is, as Dillmann severely but justly characterized it, directly repugnant to common sense. (Comm. upon Ex. Lev. p. 535), Comp. Deut. xii. 15; xv. 22. The command must have been given during the wandering in the desert. Delitzsch (Stud. 1880. No. ii. p. 65), remarks that "among the nomads butchering is an infrequent and always festive occurrence. These people live mostly upon vegetables. Such was the case with Israel. Flesh was a rarity in the first, and even in the fortieth year of their wanderings. The tabernacle was, in fact, more a place of revelation than of sacrifice. On account of the difficulty of procuring animals for sacrifice, the killing of animals for family use may have been proportionately infrequent; so much the more practicable was the law, Lev. xvii., which, from the idolatrous tendencies of the people convincingly shows itself to be a preventive law. Comp. Bredenkamp p. 129 ff., 132 ff. From a comparison of Deut. xiv. 3–20 with Lev. xi. 2–23 we draw the confident conclusion that the originality is not on the side of Deuteronomy, but that Deuteronomy has drawn either directly from Lev. xi. (Ewald, Knoble, Riehm, perhaps rightly) or from the original according to which Lev. xi. was shaped, (Dillmann). K. Marti, (Yearbook for Prot. Theol., 1880, p. 328, 331), gives us some conclusive evidence to prove that D. even in its language (*e. g.*, iv. 16–18), and in the matter of the narration (i. 23;

x. 1, 2, 22), sometimes shows dependence upon P. (Q).

Yet we must consider the language of P. As we have previously remarked, undoubtedly many archaisms have disappeared from the texts of the Hebrew Bible in the course of time, and have been replaced by later expressions; and this modernizing of the language has taken place in different books in very different degrees on account of their varying modes of usage. Conclusions therefore in regard to the time of composition on linguistic grounds can be drawn only to a limited extent, namely in such wise that one may specify a period as probably the latest, without excluding an essentially earlier origin. It is therefore, to be noted that V. Ryssel's careful but not definitive labor, " De Elohistæ (= P.) Pentateuchici sermone" (Leipsic, 1878, p. 12), has arrived at results which are incompatible with the composition of P. after the exile. We will mention here also the small but instructive composition of Delitzsch concerning the Elohistic designations of color (Mag. for Luth. Theol. 1878, pp. 590, 596; previously in English in the "Levitical Priest" by Curtiss).

i. Annexation of Deuteronomy. According to Graf's school and also many other Old Testament critics, Deuteronomy was composed shortly before the reform of Josiah. Weighty reasons oppose this view. In the first place, the account of its discovery. The high priest Hilkiah said to Shaphan, (II Kings xxii. 8), " I have found *the* book of law in the house of Jehovah." Therefore the book found, *i.e.*, the contents were not only known to him; but in his opinion, must be known to others also. The book was found in the house of Jehovah, where was its natural and designated place, (Deut. xxxi. 26). That, on the occasion perhaps of the cleaning of the holy of holies it was laid into a chamber of the temple and found there on the occasion of extensive repairs, is a supposition quite obvious and thoroughly valid; since the assumption of a forgery as we shall presently see, is impossible. The question as to the contents of the book found, will be answered very differently according to the position which the person who answers, occupies in regard to the criticism of the Pentateuch, at least in regard to the fundamental material of Deuteronomy. For from Deut. xxviii. the words of the prophetess Hulda are explained, and from the contents of Deuteronomy Josiah's reform is explained. Let us suppose that the words of the king (II Kings xxxii. 13), " because our fathers have not hearkened to the words of this book," are a bold composition of the writer of the Book of Kings, and let us suppose further that the great impression which the book immediately made upon the king, had been caused by the powerful testimony of God's spirit, and the king had no motive to inquire after the origin and the author of a writing so remarkable—yet how shall we explain the fact that the book found such a reception, so sudden, universal, and free from opposition. An external attestation must have accompanied. Hilkiah? Immediately after the new construction of Israel's history, the demand of D. to give to Levites of the province, *i. e.*, to the priests of the local sanctuaries, equal priestly rights with themselves at Jerusalem, must have been very unwelcome to the priests at Jerusalem. Nevertheless Hilkiah and the priests at Jerusalem make no opposition, raise not the least question, yes, they even assist in enforcing the new-found law; and this is conclusive evidence that there already resided in the law-book when it was found an irresistible authority. We may fairly doubt whether those mighty phrases "historically-inadmissible criterion" and "pious pragmatik" can make void all the testimonies, which the decision pronounced in the Book of Kings upon the rulers of Juda and Israel give to the earlier validity at least of the laws of Deuteronomy.

Isaiah xix. 19, "In that day shall there be an altar to the Lord in the midst of the land of Egypt and a pillar at the border thereof to the Lord." "Isaiah," say most of the later critics, and last W. Robertson Smith (O. T. P. 354), "could not bring a forbidden symbol, *e. g.*, a Mazzeba, into connection with Jehovah. This passage gives us a superior limit for the date of the code of Deuteronomy. Isaiah cannot have known the code. But in Deut. xvi. 21, 22 only idolatrous Mazzeboth, such as are worshipped, are forbidden; and this law is in harmony with the passages admitted to be old (Ex. xxiii. 24; xxxiv., 13. Comp.

also Lev. xxvi. 1). Moses himself erected twelve Mazzeboth at the altar, Ex. xxiv. 4: and so even from this point of view we gain the undoubted right to find in the proceedings of Hezekiah, (2 Kings xviii. 4) a recognition of the demand for a central sanctuary which, it has been pretended, was put forth much later, as late as the last quarter of the seventh century. Herein is a recognition of the law of Deuteronomy.

As the origin of P. in the time after the exile would be inconceivable, so Deuteronomy contains much that by no means harmonizes with the supposition that this book was written in the time of Josiah. D. speaks in friendly terms of Egypt, (xxiii. 8). How different Isaiah xxx.1ff., xxx.1; Jer. ii. 18, 36. D. speaks in a friendly way of Edom, xxiii. 8, and utters harsh words against Moab and Ammon. Just the opposite are God's words in Jeremiah's mouth, xlix. 17, 18; xlviii. 47; xlix. 6; Compare in regard to Edom, Joel iv. 19; Obad.; Isa. lxiii. 1–6. Of what use in Josiah's time would be the laws on the extermination of the Canaanites, (Deut. xx. 16–18) and the Amalekites (xxv. 17–19) and those on subjugation (xx. 10–15) and war (xx. 19–20). How can the law of Kings ch. xvii. have originated so late?

k. While Wellhausen and his followers find the code of Ezra identical with the entire Pentateuch (with the exception of a few glosses, perhaps added later), Graf, Kayser, Reuss and others take the view that Ezra has inserted only P. or its principal part. They thus avoid many rocks upon which his ship springs a leak. In place of these, other reefs endanger them. We will mention at least two of these here. If Ezra introduced only P. which, as is said, contradicts D. violently, we must assume for D. a time of concealment after the exile, which is improbable and cannot be proven. The Samaritans can hardly have received the Pent. later than Nehemiah's time. (Josephus Archæol. xi. 7, 8. Comp. Neh. xiii. 28.)

Strack closes his article with the analysis of the Pentateuch by Wellhausen and by Schrader. We omit these, as well as his copious references to the literature of this subject.

www.ingramcontent.com/pod-product-compliance
Lightning Source LLC
Chambersburg PA
CBHW020801230426

43666CB00007B/794